COOK smart

Slow Cooking

igloobooks

igloobooks

Published in 2015
by Igloo Books Ltd
Cottage Farm
Sywell
NN6 0BJ
www.igloobooks.com

Food photography and recipe development: PhotoCuisine UK
Front and back cover images © PhotoCuisine UK

LEO002 0115
2 4 6 8 10 9 7 5 3 1
ISBN 978-1-78440-154-2

Printed and manufactured in China

Contents

Soups and Light Dishes

Chicken and barley broth

Preparation time
15 minutes

Cooking time
6 hours

Serves 6

Ingredients

1 chicken carcass
2 tbsp olive oil
2 leeks, thinly sliced
2 cloves of garlic, crushed
100 g / 3 ½ oz / ½ cup pearl
    barley
½ head of broccoli, diced
½ hispi cabbage, shredded
salt and freshly ground
    black pepper

Method

1. Put the chicken carcass in a slow cooker, breaking it into pieces if it is too large, then pour over enough cold water to cover.

2. Cover and cook on low for 4 hours.

3. Towards the end of the cooking time, heat the oil in a frying pan, then fry the leeks and garlic for 5 minutes without browning.

4. Remove and discard the chicken bones, then stir the leeks and barley into the stock. Cook on medium for 1 hour 30 minutes. Stir in the broccoli and cabbage and cook for a further 30 minutes.

5. Season to taste with salt and pepper, then ladle into warm bowls to serve.

Smart tip

Rinse the barley
well before use.

Smart tip

Soak the skewers in cold water for 20 minutes before using to stop them burning.

Pepper and tomato soup with meatball skewers

Preparation time
35 minutes

Cooking time
3 hours 30 minutes

Serves 4

Ingredients

2 tbsp olive oil
1 red onion, finely chopped
1 red pepper, diced
2 cloves of garlic, crushed
1 tbsp concentrated
   tomato purée
400 g / 14 oz / 2 cups ripe
   tomatoes, peeled
   and chopped
1 litre / 1 pint 15 fl. oz / 4 cups
   vegetable stock

For the meatballs:
4 tbsp olive oil
1 onion, finely chopped
1 clove of garlic, crushed
250 g / 9 oz / 1 ⅔ cups
   coarsely minced pork
250 g / 9 oz / 1 ⅔ cups
   sausage meat
50 g / 1 ¾ oz / ⅔ cup fresh
   white breadcrumbs
½ tsp ground mace
½ tsp ground white pepper
1 egg yolk
salt and freshly ground
   black pepper

Method

1. Heat the oil in a slow cooker set to high. Stir the onion, pepper and garlic into the oil and season with salt and pepper, then cover and cook for 30 minutes, stirring every 10 minutes.

2. Stir in the tomato purée, tomatoes and stock, then cover and cook on low for 3 hours.

3. To make the meatballs, heat half of the oil in a frying pan and fry the onion for 5 minutes or until softened. Add the garlic and cook for 2 more minutes, stirring constantly, then scrape the mixture into a mixing bowl and leave to cool.

4. Add the mince, sausage meat, breadcrumbs, spices and egg yolk and mix well, then shape into grape-sized meatballs.

5. Thread the meatballs onto skewers, then heat the rest of the oil in the frying pan and cook over a low heat for 4 minutes on each side or until cooked through.

6. When the soup is ready, season to taste with salt and pepper and serve with the meatball skewers on the side.

Cauliflower and watercress soup

Preparation time
15 minutes

Cooking time
3 hours

Serves 4

Ingredients

1.2 litres / 2 pints / 4 ¾ cups
   vegetable stock
1 cauliflower, chopped
1 bay leaf
150 ml / 5 ½ fl. oz / ⅔ cup
   double (heavy) cream
3 tbsp Parmesan, finely grated
200 g / 7 oz / 6 cups
   watercress, washed
   and chopped
chunky croutons to serve
salt and freshly ground
   black pepper

Method

1. Put the stock, cauliflower and bay leaf in a slow cooker.
2. Cover and cook on low for 3 hours. Discard the bay leaf then ladle the soup into a liquidiser and blend until smooth.
3. Stir in the cream, Parmesan and watercress then season to taste with salt and pepper.
4. Pour the soup into four warm bowls and serve immediately sprinkled with chunky croutons.

Smart tip

Adding the watercress at the end will help retain freshness.

Smart tip

Vegetable stock can also be used in place of the ham stock.

Mushroom and bacon soup

Preparation time
15 minutes

Cooking time
3 hours 15 minutes

Serves 6

Ingredients

2 tbsp butter
1 leek, finely chopped
2 cloves of garlic, crushed
300 g / 10 ½ oz / 4 cups white
    button mushrooms, sliced
1 litre / 1 pint 15 fl. oz / 4 cups
    ham stock
250 ml / 7 fl. oz / 1 cup double
    (heavy) cream
salt and freshly ground
    black pepper
3 rashers bacon
croutons and chopped chervil
    to serve

Method

1. Heat the butter in a frying pan, then add the leek and
   garlic and cook without browning for 5 minutes. Stir in the
   mushrooms and cook for 5 more minutes, then scrape the
   mixture into a slow cooker and stir in the stock.

2. Cover the slow cooker and cook on low for 3 hours.

3. Stir in the cream, then use a stick blender to purée the soup
   until smooth. Season to taste with salt and pepper.

4. Grill the bacon until crisp, then cut into thin strips. Garnish the
   soup with croutons, chopped chervil and the bacon strips.

Haricot bean and vegetable soup

Preparation time
15 minutes

Cooking time
5 hours 15 minutes

Serves 4

Ingredients

200 g / 7 oz / 1 ⅓ cups dried
  haricot beans, soaked
  overnight
1 large leek, chopped
1 carrot, sliced
6 medium new potatoes,
  halved and sliced
1 courgette (zucchini), sliced
¼ savoy cabbage, shredded
salt and freshly ground
  black pepper

Method

1. Drain the beans of their soaking water, then tip them into a saucepan, cover with cold water and bring to the boil. Cook for 10 minutes, then drain well.

2. Transfer the beans to a slow cooker and stir in the rest of the ingredients along with 1 litre / 1 pint 15 fl. oz / 4 cups of water.

3. Cover the slow cooker and cook on medium for 5 hours or until the beans are tender. Season to taste with salt and pepper before serving.

Smart tip
Boiling the beans
first removes any
potential toxins.

Smart tip

Use a pair of empty mussel shells as tweezers for plucking out the mussel meat.

Curried mussel soup

Preparation time
20 minutes

Cooking time
1 hour

Serves 4

Ingredients

1 onion, finely chopped
1 red pepper, finely chopped
2 cloves of garlic, crushed
½ tbsp fresh root ginger,
    finely chopped
1 red chilli (chili), finely
    chopped
2 tsp mild curry powder
1.2 litres / 2 pints / 4 ¾ cups
    live mussels, scrubbed
500 ml / 17 ½ fl. oz / 2 cups
    fish stock
250 ml / 9 fl. oz / 1 cup double
    (heavy) cream
2 tbsp coriander (cilantro)
    leaves, chopped
1 tbsp mint leaves, chopped
salt and freshly ground
    black pepper

Method

1. Put all of the ingredients except for the cream and herbs in a slow cooker and cook on medium for 1 hour.

2. Scoop out the mussels with a slotted spoon into a bowl, then stir the cream into the soup. Cover and continue to cook while you pick the mussel meat from the shells, leaving a few whole for a garnish.

3. Stir the mussel meat into the soup with the herbs and season to taste with salt and pepper. Ladle into warm bowls and garnish with the reserved mussels in their shells.

Chunky Moroccan lamb soup

Preparation time
25 minutes

Cooking time
6 hours

Serves 6

Ingredients

450 g / 1 lb / 2 cups lamb
    shoulder, cubed
salt and freshly ground
    black pepper
2 tbsp olive oil
1 onion, finely chopped
1 large carrot, diced
2 cloves of garlic,
    finely chopped
2 tsp ras el hanout spice mix
100 g / 3 ½ oz / ¾ cup dried
    chickpeas (garbanzo beans)
100 g / 3 ½ oz / ¾ cup yellow
    split peas
600 ml / 1 pint / 2 ½ cups
    lamb or vegetable stock
400 ml / 14 fl. oz / 1 ⅔ cups
    canned plum tomatoes,
    chopped
2 tbsp coriander (cilantro)
    leaves, chopped

Method

1. Season the lamb all over with salt and pepper. Heat the oil in
   a frying pan and sear the lamb on all sides, then transfer the
   pieces to a slow cooker.

2. Fry the onion, carrot and garlic in the frying pan for 5 minutes,
   then stir in the ras el hanout. Scrape the mixture into the slow
   cooker and add the chickpeas, split peas, stock and tomatoes.

3. Cover and cook on medium for 6 hours, then season to taste
   with salt and pepper.

4. Ladle into warm bowls and serve garnished with coriander.

Smart tip

Check the soup every
2 hours and add a little
more stock or water if it
starts to thicken
too much.

Smart tip

Remove the skin of the chorizo in one piece before dicing.

Leek, potato and chorizo soup

Preparation time
25 minutes

Cooking time
6 hours

Serves 4

Ingredients

1 ham bone
2 leeks, finely chopped
450 g / 1 lb / 1 ½ cups
   potatoes, peeled
   and cubed
2 cloves of garlic, crushed
225 g / 8 oz / 1 ½ cups chorizo
   ring, diced
100 ml / 3 ½ fl. oz / ½ cup
   double (heavy) cream
salt and freshly ground
   black pepper
2 tbsp chives, finely chopped
½ tsp smoked paprika

Method

1. Put the ham bone in a slow cooker and pour over enough cold water to cover.

2. Cover and cook on low for 4 hours. Remove and discard the bone, then stir in the leeks, potato and garlic. Cover and cook on medium for 2 hours.

3. Towards the end of the cooking time, stir-fry the chorizo in a dry frying pan for 5 minutes or until crisp.

4. Transfer the soup to a liquidiser and add the double cream. Blend until smooth. Season to taste with salt and pepper, then pour into warm bowls and sprinkle over the crispy chorizo. Garnish with chives and a sprinkle of smoked paprika.

Cannellini bean and tomato soup

Preparation time
15 minutes

Cooking time
5 hours

Serves 4

Ingredients

200 g / 7 oz / 1 ⅓ cups dried
   cannellini beans,
   soaked overnight
1 onion, finely chopped
3 cloves of garlic, crushed
800 g / 1 lb 12 oz / 4 cups
   ripe tomatoes, peeled
   and chopped
400 ml / 14 fl. oz / 1 ⅔ cups
   vegetable stock
salt and freshly ground
   black pepper
1 tbsp basil leaves, shredded
1 tbsp flat leaf parsley,
   shredded

Method

1. Drain the beans of their soaking water, then tip them into a saucepan, cover with cold water and bring to the boil. Cook for 10 minutes then drain well.

2. Transfer the beans to a slow cooker and stir in the onion, garlic, tomatoes and stock.

3. Cover the slow cooker and cook on medium for 5 hours or until the beans are tender.

4. Season to taste with salt and pepper, then ladle into warm bowls and sprinkle with basil and parsley.

Smart tip
If you prefer a smooth soup, blend it in a liquidiser before serving.

Parsnip and yellow split pea soup

Preparation time
10 minutes

Cooking time
6 hours

Serves 6

Ingredients

2 tbsp olive oil
1 onion, finely chopped
1 celery stick, sliced
2 cloves of garlic, crushed
4 parsnips, peeled and diced
200 g / 7 oz / 1 ½ cups yellow
    split peas
1.2 litres / 2 pints / 5 cups
    vegetable stock
salt and freshly ground
    black pepper
6 tbsp double (heavy) cream
parsnip crisps (chips)
    to garnish

Method

1. Heat the oil in a large sauté pan and fry the onion, celery and garlic for 5 minutes or until translucent. Transfer to a slow cooker and stir in the parsnips, split peas and stock.

2. Cover and cook on medium for 6 hours, then taste the soup for seasoning and adjust with salt and pepper.

3. Ladle the soup into warm bowls, then drizzle over a little cream and garnish with parsnip crisps.

Hearty vegetable and ham soup

Preparation time
5 minutes

Cooking time
6 hours

Serves 6

Ingredients

750 g / 1 lb 10 ½ oz / 4 cups
   gammon
6 chicken wings
1 onion, finely chopped
1 celery stick, sliced
1 carrot, sliced
2 medium potatoes, peeled
   and cubed
¼ savoy cabbage, sliced
a small bunch of thyme
300 g / 10 ½ oz / 2 cups
   haricot beans,
   soaked overnight
1.2 litres / 2 pint / 5 cups
   vegetable stock
salt and freshly ground
   black pepper

Method

1. Stir all of the ingredients together in a slow cooker, then cover and cook on medium for 6 hours.

2. Remove the gammon from the slow cooker and cut it into slices, then return it to the pot.

3. Taste the soup for seasoning and adjust with salt and pepper, then ladle into warm bowls and serve.

Smart tip

Boil the beans in
unsalted water for
20 minutes, then drain
well before using.

Smart tip

Adding the avocado
after cooking helps to
retain the nutrients.

Leek, potato and avocado soup

Preparation time
10 minutes

Cooking time
4 hours

Serves 4

Ingredients

450 g / 1 lb potatoes / 1 ½ cups, peeled and cubed
2 leeks, finely chopped
2 cloves of garlic, crushed
800 ml / 1 pint 7 fl. oz / 3 ¼ cups vegetable stock
2 ripe avocados, peeled, stoned and chopped
100 ml / 3 ½ fl. oz / ½ cup double (heavy) cream
salt and freshly ground black pepper
2 tbsp chives, chopped
2 tbsp chervil leaves

Method

1. Put the potatoes, leeks, garlic and stock in a slow cooker and cook on medium for 4 hours.
2. Transfer the soup to a liquidiser with the avocados and cream and blend until smooth.
3. Season to taste with salt and pepper, then pour into warm bowls and sprinkle with chives and chervil.

Tomato and seafood soup

Preparation time
30 minutes

Cooking time
3 hours 15 minutes

Serves 6

Ingredients

2 tbsp olive oil
1 onion, finely chopped
4 cloves of garlic, crushed
800 g / 1 lb 12 ½ oz / 4 cups
  tomato passata
300 g / 10 ½ oz / 2 cups squid,
  cleaned and sliced
450 g / 1 lb / 1 ¾ cups live
  mussels, scrubbed
300 g / 10 ½ oz / 2 cups raw
  king prawns (shrimps),
  peeled
salt and freshly ground
  black pepper
flat leaf parsley and oregano
  to garnish

Method

1. Heat the oil in a frying pan and fry the onion and garlic for
   5 minutes without browning.

2. Tip the mixture into a slow cooker and stir in the passata and
   squid, then cover and cook on medium for 3 hours.

3. While the squid is cooking, heat a large saucepan over the
   hob, then tip in the mussels and 3 tbsp of water. Cover and
   cook for 5 minutes or until the mussels have all opened.
   Tip the mussels into a sieve set over a bowl to collect the
   juices, then pick out the mussel meat and discard the shells.

4. Stir the mussels and their juices into the soup along with the
   prawns. Cover and cook for another 15 minutes, then season
   to taste with salt and pepper and serve garnished with parsley
   and oregano.

Smart tip
Cooking squid long and slow gives it a melt-in-the-mouth texture.

Smart tip

Making your own chicken stock adds depth to the soup.

Chicken and sweetcorn soup

Preparation time
20 minutes

Cooking time
8 hours

Serves 6

Ingredients

4 corn on the cob
300 g / 10 ½ oz / 2 cups raw
  chicken, skinned, boned
  and diced
salt and freshly ground
  black pepper
2 tsp chilli (chili) flakes
a small bunch of chives
2 tbsp olive oil

For the stock:
1 chicken carcass
1 onion, quartered
1 carrot, roughly chopped
1 garlic bulb, halved
  horizontally
1 bay leaf

Method

1. First make the stock. Put the chicken carcass, onion, carrot, garlic and bay leaf in a slow cooker and add enough cold water to cover. Cover and cook on low for 6 hours, then pass the broth through a sieve.

2. Wash and dry the slow cooker and pour in the broth. Holding each corn cob vertically on a chopping board, cut down with a sharp knife to separate the kernels. Transfer the kernels to the slow cooker and stir in the chicken.

3. Cover the slow cooker and cook on medium for 2 hours. Ladle three quarters of the soup into a liquidiser and blend until smooth. Stir it back into the slow cooker and season to taste with salt and pepper.

4. Ladle the soup into warm bowls and garnish with chilli flakes, chives and a drizzle of olive oil.

Minestrone with gnocchi

Preparation time
5 minutes

Cooking time
2 hours 30 minutes

Serves 4

Ingredients

1 onion, chopped
2 cloves of garlic,
    finely chopped
1 carrot, diced
1 celery stick, diced
1 courgette (zucchini), diced
4 medium tomatoes, peeled
    and chopped
2 tbsp concentrated
    tomato purée
100 g / 3 ½ oz / ⅔ cup peas,
    defrosted if frozen
1.2 litres / 2 pints / 4 ¾ cups
    vegetable stock
250 g / 9 oz / 1 ½ cups potato
    gnocchi
salt and freshly ground
    black pepper
basil leaves to garnish

Method

1. Stir everything except for the gnocchi and basil together in a slow cooker and cook on medium for 2 hours.
2. Add the gnocchi and cook for a further 30 minutes or until they are all floating.
3. Season to taste with salt and pepper before ladling into warm bowls and garnishing with basil.

Smart tip
Adding the gnocchi towards the end gives them the best texture.

Smart tip

You can use this
method to poach fish
for any cold dishes.

Poached fish

Preparation time
5 minutes

Cooking time
1 hour 30 minutes

Serves 6

Ingredients

6 portions boneless fish fillet
175 ml / 6 fl. oz / ⅔ cup dry
   white wine
1 lemon, sliced
4 spring onions (scallions),
   cut into short lengths
a small bunch of thyme

Method

1. Put everything in a slow cooker and add enough cold water to cover the fish fillets.
2. Cover the slow cooker, then cook on low for 1 hour 30 minutes. Turn off the slow cooker and leave the fish to cool completely in the poaching stock.

Portuguese salt cod

Preparation time
20 minutes

Cooking time
4 hours

Serves 6

Ingredients

3 tbsp olive oil
1 onion, finely chopped
1 bulb of garlic, peeled
  and sliced
1 tsp smoked paprika
900 g / 2 lb / 6 cups ripe
  tomatoes, skinned
  and chopped
2 tbsp concentrated tomato
  purée
450 g / 1 lb / 2 ½ cups salt
  cod, soaked in cold water
  for 24 hours
freshly ground black pepper
4 tbsp flat leaf parsley,
  chopped

Method

1. Heat the oil in a frying pan and fry the onion and garlic over a low heat for 5 minutes or until softened. Stir in the paprika, then scrape the mixture into a slow cooker.

2. Add the tomatoes and tomato purée and stir well. Skin the soaked salt cod and cut it into bite-sized chunks, then stir it into the tomatoes.

3. Cover the slow cooker and cook on medium for 4 hours. Taste for seasoning – it shouldn't need any salt, but may need a little pepper. Stir in the parsley and serve.

Smart tip

Change the salt cod soaking water several times to reduce the saltiness.

Smart tip

Leaving the heads and shells on the prawns gives a stronger aromatic taste to the finished dish.

Lemon prawns and chicken wings

Preparation time
45 minutes

Cooking time
3 hours 30 minutes

Serves 4

Ingredients

4 tbsp olive oil

1 garlic clove, crushed

2 spring onions (scallions), finely chopped

1 lemon, juiced and zest finely grated

4 tbsp French tarragon, chopped

salt and freshly ground black pepper

8 chicken wings, jointed

300 g / 10 ½ oz / 1 ½ cups raw shell-on prawns (shrimps)

Method

1. Mix the oil with the garlic, spring onion, lemon juice, zest and half of the tarragon. Season the mixture with salt and pepper then massage it into the chicken wing pieces and leave to marinate for 30 minutes.

2. Heat a frying pan until smoking hot and sear the chicken wings until nicely browned. Transfer to a slow cooker with 100 ml / 3 ½ fl. oz / ½ cup of water, then cover and cook on medium for 3 hours.

3. Add the prawns and stir to coat in the juices, then cover and cook for a further 30 minutes. Season to taste before serving.

Sesame chicken and tofu

Preparation time
15 minutes

Cooking time
3 hours

Serves 4

Ingredients

2 cloves of garlic, finely
    chopped
2.5 cm (1 in) piece ginger,
    finely chopped
1 green pepper,
    cut into chunks
1 carrot, julienned
1 bunch of spring onions
    (scallions), cut into
    short lengths
75 g / 2 ½ oz / 1 cup shimeji
    mushrooms
400 ml / 14 fl. oz / 1 ⅔ cups
    chicken stock
200 ml / 7 fl. oz / ¾ cup
    coconut milk
2 chicken breasts, sliced
2 tbsp light soy sauce
2 tbsp shaoxing rice wine
1 tsp caster (superfine) sugar
2 tbsp vegetable oil
250 g / 9 oz / 1 ⅔ cups block
    of firm tofu, cubed
2 tbsp sesame seeds

Method

1. Put all of the ingredients except for the oil, tofu and sesame
   seeds in a slow cooker. Cover and cook on low for 3 hours.
2. Towards the end of the cooking time, heat the oil in a wok and
   fry the tofu until golden brown on all sides. Stir in the sesame
   seeds and cook until golden. Stir the tofu mixture into the
   slow cooker just before serving.

Smart tip

Dry the tofu really well with kitchen paper before frying to stop it spitting.

Smart tip

Ask your fishmonger to bone and cube the monkfish for you.

Monkfish curry

Preparation time
15 minutes

Cooking time
3 hours

Serves 4

Ingredients

2 tbsp sunflower oil
1 onion, thinly sliced
2 cloves of garlic, finely
  chopped
2.5 cm (1 in) piece ginger,
  finely chopped
1 red pepper, chopped
2 tbsp curry powder
4 whole mild red chillies
  (chilies)
400 ml / 14 fl. oz / 1 ⅔ cups
  fish stock
200 ml / 7 fl. oz / ¾ cup
  coconut milk
1 large monkfish tail, boned
  and cut into chunks
1 lime, juiced
salt
2 tbsp coriander (cilantro)
  leaves, shredded

Method

1. Heat the oil in a saucepan and fry the onion, garlic, ginger
   and pepper for 5 minutes. Sprinkle in the curry powder and
   fry for 1 more minute, then add the whole chillies, stock and
   coconut milk.

2. Bring the liquid to the boil, then stir in the monkfish and
   transfer everything to a slow cooker.

3. Cover and cook on medium for 3 hours. Try the sauce
   and add salt and lime juice to taste, then serve garnished
   with coriander.

Stuffed salmon with leeks

Preparation time
15 minutes

Cooking time
2 hours

Serves 4

Ingredients

600 g / 1 lb 7 oz / 4 cups
    salmon fillet
1 red pepper, diced
1 courgette (zucchini), diced
1 large tomato, diced
salt and freshly ground
    black pepper
3 leeks, julienned
250 ml / 9 fl. oz / 1 cup fish
    stock
2 tbsp dill, chopped
soured cream to serve

Method

1. Butterfly the salmon fillet and fill the cavity with the pepper, courgette and tomato. Season with salt and pepper, then fold the top back over.

2. Arrange the leeks in a slow cooker and pour over the fish stock. Lay the salmon on top, then cover with a lid and cook on low for 2 hours.

3. Cut the salmon into four portions and serve on a bed of the leeks with a little dill sprinkled over the top and soured cream on the side.

Smart tip

Tie the stuffed salmon with butchers' twine at intervals to keep the filling in.

Smart tip

Slice off and discard the rind of the pork belly before cutting it into chunks.

Pork with kidney beans

Preparation time
20 minutes

Cooking time
6 hours

Serves 8

Ingredients

400 g / 14 oz / 2 ⅔ cups dried
  kidney beans, soaked
  overnight
2 tbsp butter
450 g / 1 lb / 3 cups pork belly,
  cut into chunks
200 g / 7 oz / 1 ⅓ cups
  smoked pork sausage,
  cut into chunks
1 onion, finely chopped
4 cloves of garlic, crushed
salt and freshly ground
  black pepper
a small bunch of flat leaf
  parsley

Method

1. Drain the beans of their soaking water, then tip them into a
   saucepan, cover with cold water and bring to the boil. Cook
   for 10 minutes then drain well.

2. Meanwhile, heat the butter in a frying pan and brown the pork
   and sausage on all sides.

3. Put the beans, pork and sausage in a slow cooker with the
   onion, garlic and parsley stalks, then pour over 1 litre / 1 pint
   15 fl. oz / 4 cups of water.

4. Cover and cook on medium for 6 hours or until the beans are
   tender, but still holding their shape. Discard the parsley stalks
   and season to taste with salt and pepper.

5. Ladle into bowls, then chop the parsley leaves and sprinkle
   over the top.

Creamy sole with mussels

Preparation time
20 minutes

Cooking time
1 hour 15 minutes

Serves 4

Ingredients

4 sole fillets, skinned
2 large leeks, sliced
2 cloves of garlic, crushed
175 ml / 6 fl. oz / ⅔ cup dry
    white wine
500 ml / 17 ½ fl. oz / 2 cups
    fish stock
600 ml / 1 pint / 2 ½ cups live
    mussels, scrubbed
1 bay leaf
250 ml / 9 fl. oz / 1 cup double
    (heavy) cream
1 tsp Dijon mustard
salt and freshly ground
    black pepper
2 tbsp flat leaf parsley,
    chopped

Method

1. Roll up the sole fillets and secure with cocktail sticks.

2. Put the leeks, garlic, white wine, fish stock, mussels and bay leaf in a slow cooker and nestle the sole rolls in amongst it all. Cover and cook on medium for 1 hour.

3. Stir in the cream and mustard and cook for a further 15 minutes or until the mussels have opened. Pick out the mussel meat and discard the shells.

4. Taste and adjust the seasoning, then garnish with parsley before serving.

Smart tip
Discard any mussels
that are open
before cooking.

Smart tip

Make double the
amount and store
half in the freezer
for next time.

Tuna ragu for pasta

Preparation time
20 minutes

Cooking time
2 hours

Serves 6

Ingredients

2 tbsp olive oil
1 onion, finely chopped
1 carrot, diced
1 celery stick, diced
1 red chilli (chili), finely
   chopped
2 cloves of garlic, crushed
450 g / 1 lb / 2 cups tuna
   steak, cut into chunks
1 courgette (zucchini), sliced
400 g / 14 oz / 1 ¾ cups
   canned tomatoes, chopped
2 tbsp capers, rinsed
salt and freshly ground
   black pepper
oregano sprigs to garnish
cooked pasta to serve

Method

1. Heat the oil in a large frying pan and fry the onion, carrot and celery for 10 minutes, stirring occasionally. Add the chilli and garlic and cook for 2 minutes.

2. Scrape the vegetable mixture into a slow cooker and stir in the tuna, courgette, tomatoes and capers.

3. Cover the slow cooker and cook on medium for 2 hours.

4. Season with salt and pepper to taste and serve with pasta, garnished with oregano sprigs.

Salt cod with shrimp and vegetable sauce

Preparation time
20 minutes

Cooking time
2 hours

Serves 4

Ingredients

4 portions of salt cod, soaked
  in cold water for 24 hours
1 red onion, finely chopped
1 orange pepper, diced
1 courgette (zucchini), diced
75 g / 2 ½ oz / 1 cup
  mushrooms, diced
1 tsp cornflour (cornstarch)
2 tsp grain mustard
100 g / 3 ½ oz / 1 cup brown
  shrimps, peeled
boiled potatoes to serve

Method

1. Arrange the salt cod portions in a slow cooker, then scatter the onion, pepper, courgette and mushrooms over the top.
2. Pour over enough boiling water to just cover the fish, then put on the lid and cook on medium for 2 hours.
3. Strain the cooking stock into a saucepan and bring to the boil. Slake the cornflour in 1 tbsp of cold water, then stir it into the sauce to thicken. Stir in the mustard and shrimps and taste for seasoning, then stir in the vegetables from the slow cooker.
4. Serve the salt cod with the shrimp and vegetable sauce with some plain boiled potatoes on the side.

Smart tip
Drain and rinse the salt cod before using.

Smart tip

Try adding a handful of olives or capers after cooking for an authentic Mediterranean taste.

Ratatouille

Preparation time
5 minutes

Cooking time
4 hours

Serves 6

Ingredients

1 aubergine (eggplant), cubed
2 courgettes (zucchinis), sliced
1 red pepper, deseeded
    and cubed
1 yellow pepper, deseeded
    and cubed
2 large tomatoes, cubed
1 large onion, sliced
2 cloves of garlic, crushed
3 tbsp olive oil
150 ml / 5 ½ fl. oz / ⅔ cup dry
    white wine
150 ml / 5 ½ fl. oz / ⅔ cup
    tomato passata
salt and freshly ground
    black pepper

Method

1. Mix all of the ingredients together in a slow cooker and
   season with salt and pepper.
2. Cover the slow cooker and cook on medium for 4 hours,
   stirring halfway through.
3. Taste again for seasoning and add more salt or pepper
   if needed.

Stews and Casseroles

Chicken, rice and vegetable stew

Preparation time
5 minutes

Cooking time
4 hours

Serves 6

Ingredients

6 chicken thighs, skinned,
  boned and cubed
1 onion, finely chopped
1 celery stick, finely chopped
2 carrots, cut into chunks
1 tsp dried herbs de Provence
200 g / 7 oz / 1 cup long
  grain rice
800 ml / 1 pint 7 fl. oz / 3 ¼
  cups chicken stock
salt and freshly ground
  black pepper
flat leaf parsley to garnish

Method

1. Mix all of the ingredients except for the parsley together in a
   slow cooker. Cover and cook on medium for 4 hours.
2. Season to taste with salt and pepper and garnish with flat leaf
   parsley before serving.

Smart tip

Rinse the rice under
running water
before using.

Smart tip

Baby onions are sometimes labelled as pickling onions.

Creamy veal and wild mushroom casserole

Preparation time
10 minutes

Cooking time
4 hours 30 minutes

Serves 4

Ingredients

800 g / 1 lb 12 oz / 4 ¾ cups
  veal shoulder, cubed
450 g / 1 lb / 2 cups baby
  onions, peeled
1 celery stick, finely chopped
1 clove of garlic, crushed
600 ml / 1 pint / 2 ½ cups light
  veal or chicken stock
300 ml / 10 ½ fl. oz / 1 ¼ cups
  double (heavy) cream
salt and freshly ground
  black pepper
2 tbsp butter
150 g / 5 ½ oz / 2 cups wild
  mushrooms, chopped
  if large
2 tbsp chervil, chopped

Method

1. Put the veal, onions, celery, garlic and stock in a slow cooker and stir well to mix.

2. Cook on low for 4 hours. Stir in the cream and season to taste with salt and pepper, then cook on high for 30 minutes.

3. Meanwhile, heat the butter in a frying pan and sauté the mushrooms for 5 minutes or until golden.

4. Stir the mushrooms into the casserole and serve, garnished with chervil.

Salmon and butter bean blanquette

Preparation time
15 minutes

Cooking time
7 hours 10 minutes

Serves 6

Ingredients

300 g / 10 ½ oz / 2 cups
dried butter beans,
soaked overnight
1 onion, quartered
2 carrots, halved
2 celery sticks, halved
1 bulb of garlic, halved
horizontally
2 bay leaves
2 tbsp butter
2 leeks, halved and sliced
salt and white pepper
200 ml / 7 fl. oz / ¾ cup
double (heavy) cream
900 g / 2 lb / 6 cups salmon
fillet, skinned
2 tbsp basil, shredded

Method

1. Drain the beans of their soaking water, then tip them into a saucepan, cover with cold water and bring to the boil. Cook for 10 minutes, then drain well.

2. Tip the beans into a slow cooker and stir in the onion, carrots, celery, garlic, bay leaves and 1 litre / 1 pint 15 fl. oz / 4 cups of water. Cover and cook on medium for 6 hours.

3. Towards the end of the cooking time, heat the butter in a saucepan and gently fry the leeks for 10 minutes or until softened.

4. Drain the butter beans, reserving the cooking stock, and discard the vegetables. Put the beans back into the slow cooker and stir in the leeks, cream and enough of the cooking stock to just cover them. Season to taste with salt and white pepper.

5. Cut the salmon fillet into bite-sized chunks and stir them in, then cover the slow cooker and cook on low for 1 hour.

6. Ladle the blanquette into bowls and garnish with basil.

Smart tip

Any leftover bean cooking stock can be used as vegetable stock for soups.

Smart tip

Ask your butcher
for farmed rabbits,
which are plumper
and juicier.

Rabbit in mustard sauce

Preparation time
10 minutes

Cooking time
3 hours 30 minutes

Serves 6

Ingredients

2 rabbits, jointed
1 leek, finely chopped
3 cloves of garlic, crushed
600 ml / 1 pint / 2 ½ cups
    chicken stock
300 ml / 10 ½ fl. oz / 1 ¼ cups
    double (heavy) cream
1 tbsp Dijon mustard
salt and freshly ground
    black pepper
2 tbsp basil leaves, shredded

Method

1. Put everything except for the mustard and basil in a slow cooker and stir well to mix.

2. Cook on low for 3 hours, then remove the rabbit pieces from the cooker with a slotted spoon.

3. Shred the meat and discard the bones, then stir the rabbit back into the slow cooker with the cream and mustard. Cover and cook on high for 30 minutes, then season to taste with salt and pepper.

4. Garnish with shredded basil and serve.

Coq au vin

Preparation time
20 minutes

Cooking time
5 hours

Serves 4

Ingredients

1 medium chicken, jointed
salt and freshly ground
   black pepper
3 tbsp plain (all-purpose) flour
1 tsp mustard powder
3 tbsp olive oil
2 tbsp butter
150 g / 5 ½ oz / 1 cup
   pancetta, cubed
200 g / 7 oz / 1 ⅓ cups baby
   onions, peeled
600 ml / 1 pint / 2 ½ cups
   red wine
150 g / 5 ½ oz / 2 cups button
   mushrooms, quartered

Method

1. Season the chicken well with salt and pepper, then toss with the flour and mustard powder to coat.
2. Heat half of the oil and butter in a sauté pan and sear the chicken pieces on all sides.
3. Remove the chicken from the pan and add the rest of the oil and butter, followed by the pancetta and onions. Sauté for 5 minutes, then pour in the wine and bring to a simmer.
4. Scrape the mixture into a slow cooker and add the seared chicken. Cover and cook on low for 4 hours, then stir in the mushrooms and cook for 1 more hour.
5. Taste and adjust the seasoning with salt and pepper before serving.

Smart tip

Try blanching the onions in boiling water for 30 seconds to make them easier to peel.

Smart tip

Look out for rose veal which is farmed to higher animal welfare standards.

Veal and spinach blanquette

Preparation time
10 minutes

Cooking time
4 hours 30 minutes

Serves 4

Ingredients

800 g / 1 lb 12 oz / 4 ¾ cups
    veal fillet, sliced
1 leek, finely chopped
1 celery stick, finely chopped
1 clove of garlic, crushed
1 tsp caraway seeds
600 ml / 1 pint / 2 ½ cups light
    veal or chicken stock
300 ml / 10 ½ fl. oz / 1 ¼ cups
    double (heavy) cream
salt and freshly ground
    black pepper
100 g / 3 ½ oz / 3 cups baby
    leaf spinach, washed

Method

1. Put everything except for the cream and spinach in a slow
   cooker and stir well to mix.
2. Cook on low for 4 hours. Stir in the cream and season to taste
   with salt and pepper, then cook on high for 30 minutes.
3. Stir in the spinach and leave to wilt for 1 minute, then serve.

Beef, chorizo and mushroom stew

Preparation time
20 minutes

Cooking time
6 hours

Serves 6

Ingredients

450 g / 1 lb / 3 cups chuck
   steak, cut into large chunks
salt and freshly ground
   black pepper
2 tbsp plain (all-purpose) flour
2 tbsp olive oil
1 chorizo ring, sliced
   diagonally
3 cloves of garlic, chopped
2 bay leaves
700 ml / 1 pint 3 ½ fl. oz / 2 ¾
   cups beef stock
225 g / 8 oz / 3 cups baby
   button mushrooms
rocket (arugula) leaves
   to garnish

Method

1. Season the beef with salt and pepper and dust the pieces
   with flour to coat. Heat the oil in a large frying pan and sear
   the beef in batches on all sides. Transfer the beef to a slow
   cooker, then sear the chorizo pieces on both sides and add
   them to the beef.

2. Stir the garlic, bay leaves and stock into the slow cooker, then
   cover and cook on low for 5 hours.

3. Stir in the mushrooms, then cover and cook for another hour.

4. Season to taste with salt and pepper before serving,
   garnished with rocket leaves.

Smart tip

Adding the mushrooms towards the end means they retain their texture.

Smart tip

Remove the bay
leaves and thyme after
cooking and garnish
with fresh herbs.

Basque chicken

Preparation time
15 minutes

Cooking time
6 hours

Serves 4

Ingredients

1 small chicken, jointed
salt and freshly ground
    black pepper
2 tbsp plain (all-purpose) flour
2 tbsp olive oil
1 onion, finely chopped
3 cloves of garlic, crushed
3 carrots, peeled and cut into
    short lengths
2 red peppers, cut into chunks
3 medium tomatoes, cut
    into chunks
2 tbsp concentrated
    tomato purée
2 bay leaves
a small bunch of thyme
1 tsp smoked paprika
175 ml / 6 fl. oz / ⅔ cup dry
    white wine
500 ml / 17 ½ fl. oz / 2 cups
    chicken stock

Method

1. Season the chicken with salt and pepper and dust the pieces with flour to coat. Heat the oil in a large frying pan and sear the chicken on all sides.

2. Transfer the chicken to a slow cooker and stir in the rest of the ingredients.

3. Cover the slow cooker and cook on low for 6 hours, stirring every 2 hours. Season with salt and pepper before serving.

Seafood and vegetable stew

Preparation time
15 minutes

Cooking time
1 hour

Serves 4

Ingredients

3 tbsp olive oil
1 onion, chopped
2 carrots, peeled and sliced
2 cloves of garlic, crushed
175 ml / 6 fl. oz / ⅔ cup dry
  white wine
a pinch of saffron
500 ml / 17 ½ fl. oz / 2 cups
  fish stock
3 tbsp concentrated
  tomato purée
600 ml / 1 pint / 2 ½ cups live
  mussels, scrubbed
12 king prawns (shrimps),
  heads removed
1 large monkfish tail, boned
  and cut into chunks
150 g / 5 ½ oz / 1 cup peas,
  defrosted if frozen

Method

1. Heat the oil in a sauté pan and fry the onion and carrots for 5 minutes to soften without browning. Add the garlic and cook for 1 more minute, then pour in the wine and reduce by half.

2. Stir in the saffron, stock and tomato purée and bring to a simmer, then transfer the contents of the pan to a slow cooker and stir in the mussels, prawns, monkfish and peas.

3. Cover the slow cooker and cook on medium for 1 hour or until all of the mussels have opened.

Smart tip

Tie the prawn heads in a square of muslin cloth and cook in the stew for a stronger taste.

Smart tip
Try to re-cover the
cooker quickly after
stirring to stop the
temperature from
dropping too much.

Beef, pepper and olive stew

Preparation time
15 minutes

Cooking time
6 hours

Serves 4

Ingredients

450 g / 1 lb / 3 cups stewing
   beef, cubed
2 tbsp plain (all-purpose) flour
2 tbsp olive oil
1 red pepper, cut into wedges
1 yellow pepper,
   cut into wedges
1 green pepper,
   cut into wedges
150 g / 5 ½ oz / 1 cup green
   olives, pitted
1 onion, finely chopped
3 cloves of garlic, crushed
2 tbsp concentrated
   tomato purée
2 bay leaves
a few sprigs of thyme
500 ml / 17 ½ fl. oz / 2 cups
   good quality beef stock
salt and freshly ground
   black pepper
couscous to serve

Method

1. Season the beef with salt and pepper and dust the pieces with flour to coat. Heat the oil in a large frying pan and sear the beef in batches on all sides.

2. Transfer the beef to a slow cooker and stir in the rest of the ingredients, except the couscous. Season well with salt and pepper.

3. Cover the slow cooker and cook on low for 6 hours, stirring every 2 hours. Serve with couscous.

Turkey blanquette

Preparation time
15 minutes

Cooking time
4 hours

Serves 6

Ingredients

2 tbsp butter
800 g / 1 lb 12 oz / 5 cups
    turkey breast, cubed
2 tbsp plain (all-purpose) flour
1 leek, finely chopped
2 carrots, julienned
2 courgettes (zucchinis),
    julienned
600 ml / 1 pint / 2 ½ cups light
    veal or chicken stock
300 ml / 10 ½ fl. oz / 1 ¼ cups
    double (heavy) cream
salt and freshly ground
    black pepper
2 tbsp curly parsley, chopped

Method

1. Heat the butter in a frying pan. Dust the turkey pieces with flour and season with salt and pepper, then sear them all over.
2. Transfer the turkey to a slow cooker and mix with the rest of the ingredients, except for the parsley.
3. Cook on low for 4 hours, then taste the sauce for seasoning and adjust with salt and black pepper. Stir in the parsley and serve.

Smart tip

Flouring the turkey pieces helps to thicken the sauce later in the cooking process.

Smart tip

The garlic cloves can be peeled at the table to reveal the delicious garlic purée within.

Chickpea and chorizo tapas

Preparation time
30 minutes

Cooking time
3 hours

Serves 4

Ingredients

300 g / 10 ½ oz / 2 cups
dried chickpeas (garbanzo
beans), soaked overnight
1 bulb of garlic, separated
into cloves
3 tbsp olive oil
1 onion, finely chopped
225 g / 8 oz / 1 cup chorizo
ring, thickly sliced
200 g / 7 oz / ¾ cup canned
tomatoes, chopped
salt and freshly ground
black pepper
2 tbsp flat leaf parsley,
shredded

Method

1. Drain the chickpeas of their soaking water and put them in a
large saucepan of cold water. Bring to the boil and cook for
10 minutes, then drain well.

2. Transfer the chickpeas to a slow cooker with the garlic, then
pour in 1.5 litres / 3 pints / 6 cups of water. Cover and cook on
high for 3 hours or until the chickpeas are tender.

3. Towards the end of the cooking time, heat the oil in a large
sauté pan and fry the onion for 5 minutes. Add the chorizo
to the pan and sauté for a further 5 minutes, then add the
tomatoes. Simmer for 15 minutes or until well reduced.

4. When the chickpeas are ready, drain them, retaining a cupful
of the cooking stock, and stir the chickpeas and garlic into the
tomato sauce. Add a little of the reserved cooking stock if the
mixture looks too dry, or simmer for a further 10 minutes if it
looks too runny.

5. Season to taste with salt and pepper then serve garnished
with parsley.

Stewed peppers and tomatoes

Preparation time
5 minutes

Cooking time
3 hours 30 minutes

Serves 4

Ingredients

3 tbsp olive oil
1 onion, sliced
2 red peppers, cut into chunks
2 yellow peppers,
    cut into chunks
2 green peppers,
    cut into chunks
salt and freshly ground
    black pepper
2 cloves of garlic, sliced
4 medium tomatoes, halved
4 tbsp dry sherry
250 ml / 9 fl. oz / 1 cup
    vegetable stock

Method

1. Put the oil in a slow cooker and heat on high. Stir in the onion and peppers and season with salt and pepper. Cover and cook for 1 hour 30 minutes, stirring every 15 minutes.

2. Stir in the garlic, tomatoes and sherry, then pour over the vegetable stock.

3. Cover and cook on low for 2 hours. Season to taste before serving.

Smart tip

This recipe also makes a delicious soup – purée in a liquidiser until smooth.

Smart tip

Sear the rabbit until golden brown for the best results.

Rabbit with baby onions

Preparation time
30 minutes

Cooking time
3 hours

Serves 4

Ingredients

1 large rabbit, jointed
salt and freshly ground black
    pepper
3 tbsp plain (all-purpose) flour
1 tsp mustard powder
3 tbsp olive oil
2 tbsp butter
450 g / 1 lb / 3 cups baby
    onions, peeled
3 cloves of garlic, crushed
600 ml / 1 pint / 2 ½ cups dry
    white wine
2 tbsp white wine vinegar
2 tbsp runny honey
1 tbsp Dijon mustard
4 star anise
3 bay leaves
chopped flat leaf parsley
    to garnish

Method

1. Season the rabbit well with salt and pepper, then toss with the flour and mustard powder to coat.

2. Heat half of the oil and butter in a sauté pan and sear the rabbit pieces on all sides.

3. Remove the rabbit from the pan and add the rest of the oil and butter, followed by the onions. Sauté for 5 minutes, then add the garlic and cook for 1 more minute. Pour in the wine and bring to a simmer.

4. Scrape the mixture into a slow cooker and add the seared rabbit and the rest of the ingredients, except the parsley. Cover and cook on low for 3 hours.

5. Taste and adjust the seasoning with salt and pepper, then serve, garnished with parsley.

Pear, chickpea and vegetable stew

Preparation time
25 minutes

Cooking time
3 hours 30 minutes

Serves 4

Ingredients

200 g / 7 oz / 1 ⅓ cups dried chickpeas (garbanzo beans), soaked overnight
1 onion, finely chopped
1 carrot, cut into chunks
½ small squash, peeled and cut into chunks
6 white asparagus spears, cut into short lengths
¼ savoy cabbage, shredded
1 orange, juiced and zest finely grated
2 pears, halved and cored
1 tbsp melted butter
salt and freshly ground black pepper
2 tbsp flat leaf parsley, chopped

Method

1. Drain the chickpeas of their soaking water, then tip them into a saucepan, cover with cold water and bring to the boil. Cook for 10 minutes then drain well.

2. Transfer the chickpeas to a slow cooker and stir in the onion, carrot, squash, asparagus, cabbage, orange juice and zest and 300 ml / 10 fl. oz / 1 ¼ cups of water.

3. Cover the slow cooker and cook on high for 3 hours or until the chickpeas are tender.

4. Brush the cut side of the pears with melted butter and sear on a hot griddle pan until nicely marked. Season the vegetable mixture with salt and pepper, then add the pears and cook for another 30 minutes. Garnish with parsley before serving.

Smart tip

Don't add any salt until the chickpeas are tender or they will remain hard.

Smart tip
Adding the sugar cubes
at the end enriches
the sauce.

Topside with caramelised onions

Preparation time
35 minutes

Cooking time
6 hours

Serves 6

Ingredients

900 g / 2 lb / 6 cups topside of beef

salt and freshly ground black pepper

4 tbsp olive oil

3 onions, sliced

2 bay leaves

1 tbsp concentrated tomato purée

700 ml / 1 pint 3 ½ fl. oz / 2 ¾ cups dark ale

a small bunch of thyme, plus extra to garnish

4 brown sugar cubes

Method

1. Season the beef all over with salt and pepper. Heat 2 tbsp of the oil in a large sauté pan and sear the beef on all sides. Transfer the beef to a slow cooker.

2. Heat the rest of the oil in the sauté pan then fry the onions and bay leaves over a gentle heat for 15 minutes, stirring occasionally, until caramelised.

3. Stir in the tomato purée, ale and thyme and bring to the boil, then pour the mixture over the beef.

4. Cover the slow cooker and cook on medium for 6 hours or until the beef is really tender. Stir the sugar cubes into the sauce, then season to taste with salt and pepper.

5. Garnish with extra thyme before carving and serving.

Lamb chops with tomato and mushroom stew

Preparation time
15 minutes

Cooking time
2 hours

Serves 4

Ingredients

4 tbsp olive oil
8 lamb chops
4 rashers back bacon
2 bulbs of fennel, thickly sliced
1 onion, sliced
1 tbsp rosemary leaves
150 g / 5 ½ oz / 2 cups button
    mushrooms, sliced
100 ml / 3 ½ fl. oz / ½ cup dry
    white wine
400 ml / 7 fl. oz / 1 ⅔ cups
    tomato passata
a few sprigs of basil

Method

1. Heat the oil in a frying pan and sear the lamb chops on both sides, followed by the bacon. Transfer to a slow cooker and add the rest of the ingredients.
2. Cover and cook on high for 2 hours, then garnish with basil and serve.

Smart tip

Searing the lamb first seals in the juices and improves the taste of the finished dish.

Smart tip
Use bone-in chicken
thighs for the best taste
and texture.

Chicken, lemon and olive stew

Preparation time
5 minutes

Cooking time
4 hours

Serves 6

Ingredients

6 chicken thighs, skinned
6 medium waxy potatoes,
 peeled
2 onions, sliced
4 cloves of garlic, chopped
1 preserved lemon,
 rind only, sliced
75 g / 2 ½ oz / ½ cup green
 olives, pitted
400 ml / 14 fl. oz / 1 ⅔ cups
 chicken stock
salt and freshly ground
 black pepper
½ tsp paprika
a few sprigs of coriander
 (cilantro)

Method

1. Mix all of the ingredients except for the paprika and coriander together in a slow cooker. Cover and cook on medium for 4 hours or until the chicken and potatoes are tender.

2. Season to taste with salt and pepper, then garnish with a sprinkle of paprika and a few sprigs of coriander.

Pork and carrot stew

Preparation time
15 minutes

Cooking time
6 hours

Serves 4

Ingredients

450 g / 1 lb / 3 cups pork
    shoulder, cubed
salt and freshly ground
    black pepper
2 tbsp plain (all-purpose) flour
2 tbsp olive oil
1 onion, finely chopped
3 cloves of garlic, crushed
450 g / 1 lb / 2 ½ cups carrots,
    peeled and cut into
    short lengths
2 tbsp concentrated
    tomato purée
2 bay leaves
2 cinnamon sticks
500 ml / 17 ½ fl. oz / 2 cups
    tomato passata

Method

1. Season the pork with salt and pepper and dust the pieces
   with flour to coat. Heat the oil in a large frying pan and sear
   the pork in batches on all sides.
2. Transfer the pork to a slow cooker and stir in the rest of
   the ingredients.
3. Cover the slow cooker and cook on low for 6 hours, stirring
   every 2 hours. Season with salt and pepper before serving.

Smart tip

Add a drop of water if the sauce gets too thick whilst cooking.

Smart tip

When corn on the cob is out of season, use frozen sweetcorn kernels instead.

Chorizo, potato and sweetcorn stew

Preparation time
5 minutes

Cooking time
3 hours

Serves 4

Ingredients

250 g / 9 oz / 1 ⅔ cups mini
   cooking chorizo
1 large potato,
   cut into wedges
2 corn cobs, cut into
   thick slices
4 spring onions (scallions),
   cut into short lengths
1 chipotle chilli (chili)
400 ml / 7 fl. oz / 1 ⅔ cups
   tomato passata
1 lime, cut into chunks
2 tbsp coriander (cilantro),
   chopped

Method

1. Mix all of the ingredients together, except for the lime and coriander, in a slow cooker.

2. Cover and cook on medium for 3 hours or until the potatoes are tender, but still holding their shape.

3. Spoon into warm bowls and garnish with lime chunks and coriander.

Pork, potato and flageolet stew

Preparation time
20 minutes

Cooking time
6 hours

Serves 6

Ingredients

150 g / 5 ½ oz / 1 cup dried
   flageolet beans,
   soaked overnight
150 g / 5 ½ oz / 1 cup dried
   chickpeas (garbanzo
   beans), soaked overnight
450 g / 1 lb / 3 cups pork
   shoulder, cut into chunks
2 medium potatoes, sliced
2 carrots, chopped
1 onion, finely chopped
4 cloves of garlic, chopped
400 ml / 14 fl. oz / 1 ⅔ cups
   chicken stock
400 ml / 14 fl. oz / 1 ⅔ cups
   tomato passata
salt and freshly ground
   black pepper
100 g / 3 ½ oz / 4 cups
   spinach, washed

Method

1. Drain the beans and chickpeas from their soaking water and put them in a large saucepan of cold water. Bring to the boil and cook for 10 minutes, then drain well.

2. Mix the beans with the rest of the ingredients, except for the spinach, in a slow cooker. Cover and cook on medium for 6 hours or until the pulses are tender, but still holding their shape.

3. Season to taste with salt and pepper, then stir in the spinach, cover the pan and leave to wilt for 5 minutes.

Smart tip

Adding the spinach at the last minute retains the fresh taste and nutrients.

Smart tip

Remove the ink sacs from the squid carefully to avoid staining.

Seafood, orange and vegetable stew

Preparation time
5 minutes

Cooking time
2 hours 30 minutes

Serves 6

Ingredients

450 g / 1 lb / 2 cups cod fillet, cubed
2 squid, cleaned and sliced
2 shallots, sliced
2 cloves of garlic, crushed
175 ml / 6 fl. oz / ⅔ cup dry white wine
500 ml / 17 ½ fl. oz / 2 cups fish stock
1 orange, juiced and zest finely grated
250 ml / 9 fl. oz / 1 cup double (heavy) cream
½ cucumber, sliced
½ head of broccoli, chopped
100 g / 3 ½ oz / 1 cup sugar snap peas, trimmed
salt and freshly ground black pepper

Method

1. Put the cod, squid, shallots, garlic, wine, stock and orange juice and zest in a slow cooker and cook on low for 2 hours.

2. Stir in the cream and vegetables, then replace the lid and cook for a further 30 minutes. Season to taste with salt and pepper before serving.

Mediterranean lamb

Preparation time
20 minutes

Cooking time
5 hours 30 minutes

Serves 6

Ingredients

900 g / 2 lb / 6 cups lamb leg,
  cut into large chunks
salt and freshly ground
  black pepper
2 tbsp plain (all-purpose) flour
2 tbsp olive oil
125 ml / 4 ½ fl. oz / ½ cup
  white wine
6 medium potatoes, peeled
  and cut into large chunks
2 onions, thickly sliced
2 red peppers, deseeded
  and sliced
4 cloves of garlic, crushed
a few sprigs of thyme, plus
  extra to garnish
500 ml / 17 ½ fl. oz / 2 cups
  good quality lamb stock
4 tbsp kalamata olives

Method

1. Season the lamb with salt and pepper and dust with flour to coat. Heat the oil in a large frying pan and sear the lamb on all sides.

2. Transfer the lamb to a slow cooker, then deglaze the pan with the wine and scrape it in with the lamb. Add the potatoes, onions, peppers, garlic, thyme and stock to the slow cooker and season well with salt and pepper.

3. Put the lid on the slow cooker and cook on low for 5 hours. Stir in the olives, then cover and cook for another 30 minutes. Serve garnished with fresh thyme sprigs.

Smart tip

Choose waxy potatoes that won't break down during cooking.

Smart tip

Adding the chorizo and preserved lemon at the end helps to retain their texture and aroma.

Chorizo, bean and squash stew

Preparation time
20 minutes

Cooking time
6 hours 10 minutes

Serves 4

Ingredients

2 tbsp olive oil
1 large onion, chopped
2 cloves of garlic, crushed
½ small butternut squash,
    peeled and cubed
1 tsp smoked paprika
300 ml / 10 ½ fl. oz / 1 ¼ cups
    tomato passata
200 ml / 7 fl. oz / ¾ cup
    vegetable stock
1 Romano pepper, sliced
200 g / 7 oz / 1 ⅓ cups dried
    cannellini beans,
    soaked overnight
1 preserved lemon
100 g / 3 ½ oz / ⅔ cup chorizo
    slices, cut into thick ribbons
salt and freshly ground
    black pepper
a small bunch of flat
    leaf parsley

Method

1. Heat the oil in a large saucepan and fry the onion for
   5 minutes, stirring occasionally. Add the garlic, squash and
   paprika and cook for 2 minutes, then scrape the mixture
   into a slow cooker.

2. Pour in the passata and vegetable stock and add the pepper
   and cannellini beans, then cover and cook on medium for
   6 hours.

3. Cut the preserved lemon into quarters then use a teaspoon
   to scrape away and discard the flesh. Rinse the rind then cut
   it into long thin strips and add to the slow cooker with the
   chorizo, then cover and cook for 10 more minutes.

4. Season the stew to taste with salt and pepper then ladle into
   warm bowls and sprinkle with parsley leaves.

Vegetable tagine

Preparation time
5 minutes

Cooking time
4 hours

Serves 4

Ingredients

3 courgettes (zucchinis),
    cut into chunks
1 aubergine (eggplant),
    cut into chunks
2 red peppers, cut into chunks
1 onion, finely chopped
3 cloves of garlic,
    finely chopped
400 g / 14 oz / 1 ¾ cups
    canned tomatoes, chopped
2 tsp ras el hanout spice mix
1 tbsp thyme leaves
salt and freshly ground
    black pepper

Method

1. Stir everything together in a slow cooker with a big pinch of salt.
2. Cover the slow cooker and cook on medium for 4 hours.
3. Season to taste with salt and pepper, then decant into four individual serving tagines.

Smart tip

Warm the tagines
in a low oven
before filling and
serving.

Smart tip

Warm the pumpkin shells for 1 minute in the microwave to stop the stew from going cold.

Beef and pumpkin stew

Preparation time
25 minutes

Cooking time
6 hours

Serves 4

Ingredients

5 small culinary pumpkins
450 g / 1 lb / 3 cups stewing
    beef, cubed
4 tbsp plain (all-purpose) flour
2 tbsp olive oil
1 onion, chopped
1 celery stick, cut into chunks
3 cloves of garlic, crushed
2 tbsp concentrated
    tomato purée
½ tsp ground cumin
½ tsp ground paprika
500 ml / 17 ½ fl. oz / 2 cups
    good quality beef stock
salt and freshly ground
    black pepper
3 tbsp pistachio nuts, chopped
a few sprigs of coriander
    (cilantro) to serve

Method

1. Slice the tops off the pumpkins, then scrape out and discard the seeds. Peel one of the pumpkins and cut the flesh into chunks.

2. Toss the beef in the flour and season with salt and pepper. Heat the oil in a frying pan, then sear the beef in batches on all sides.

3. Transfer the beef to a slow cooker and stir in the pumpkin chunks, onion, celery, garlic, tomato purée, spices and beef stock. Cover and cook on medium for 6 hours, then season to taste with salt and pepper.

4. Spoon the stew into the cavities of the other four pumpkins and garnish with chopped pistachios and coriander sprigs.

Pies and Bakes

Ragu pasta bake

Preparation time
30 minutes

Cooking time
5 hours

Serves 4

Ingredients

3 tbsp olive oil
1 onion, finely chopped
1 red pepper, diced
1 large carrot, diced
4 cloves of garlic, crushed
2 red chillies (chilies), sliced
450 g / 1 lb / 3 cups minced
  beef
2 tbsp concentrated
  tomato purée
200 ml / 7 fl. oz / ¾ cup red
  wine
400 ml / 14 fl. oz / 1 ½ cups
  beef stock
50 g / 1 ¾ oz / ⅓ cup black
  olives, pitted and chopped
salt and freshly ground
  black pepper
400 g / 14 oz / 2 ½ cups dried
  penne pasta
75 g / 2 ½ oz / ¾ cup Cheddar
  cheese, grated
chopped flat leaf parsley
  to garnish

Method

1. Heat the oil in a large frying pan and fry the onion, pepper, carrot, garlic and chillies for 5 minutes, stirring occasionally. Add the mince and fry until it starts to brown, then stir in the tomato purée.

2. Pour in the wine and boil rapidly for 2 minutes, then scrape everything into a slow cooker with the beef stock and olives.

3. Cover the slow cooker and cook on medium for 5 hours, then season with salt and pepper to taste.

4. Towards the end of the cooking time, cook the pasta in boiling salted water according to the packet instructions or until al dente. Drain well, then stir it into the ragu.

5. Cover the top with grated cheese, then melt it under a hot grill. Garnish with parsley and serve immediately.

Smart tip

Browning the mince first gives a better taste to the finished dish.

Smart tip
Ricing the potato into the hot milk gives mash the best texture.

Beef stew with potato gratin topping

Preparation time
35 minutes

Cooking time
6 hours

Serves 4

Ingredients

450 g / 1 lb / 3 cups chuck
    steak, cut into large chunks
salt and freshly ground
    black pepper
4 tbsp plain (all-purpose) flour
2 tbsp butter
1 onion, finely chopped
2 carrots, cut into chunks
¼ white cabbage, sliced
2 bay leaves
1 tbsp Worcestershire sauce
700 ml / 1 pint 3 ½ fl. oz / 2 ¾
    cups Irish stout
flat leaf parsley to garnish

For the topping:
900 g / 2 lb / 3 ½ cups Desiree
    potatoes, peeled
    and cubed
200 g / 7 oz / ¾ cup butter,
    cubed
100 ml / 3 ½ oz / ½ cup milk
1 tbsp grain mustard

Method

1. Season the beef with salt and pepper and dust the pieces with flour to coat. Heat the butter in a large frying pan and sear the beef in batches on all sides.

2. Transfer the beef to a slow cooker and stir in the onion, carrots, cabbage, bay leaves, Worcestershire sauce and stout.

3. Put the lid on the slow cooker and cook on low for 6 hours, stirring every 2 hours. Season to taste with salt and pepper.

4. To make the topping, cook the potatoes in boiling salted water for 12 minutes or until tender. Tip the potatoes into a colander and leave to drain.

5. Put the saucepan back on the heat, add the butter, milk and mustard and bring to a simmer. Use a potato ricer to crush the potatoes straight into the hot milk, then briefly beat the mixture with a wooden spoon until smooth.

6. Spoon the potato on top of the stew then lightly brown the top under a hot grill before serving, garnished with parsley.

Vegetable bake

Preparation time
15 minutes

Cooking time
4 hours

Serves 4

Ingredients

450 g / 1 lb / 2 cups
   vegetarian mince
1 onion, finely chopped
1 green pepper, diced
1 fennel bulb, diced
3 cloves of garlic, sliced
250 ml / 9 fl. oz / 1 cup
   vegetable stock
salt and freshly ground
   black pepper
2 courgettes (zucchinis)
1 mozzarella ball, diced
150 ml / 5 ½ fl. oz / ⅔ cup
   double (heavy) cream
2 tbsp basil leaves, chopped
1 tbsp flat leaf parsley,
   chopped

Method

1. Stir the vegetarian mince, onion, pepper, fennel, garlic and stock together in a slow cooker.
2. Cover the slow cooker and cook on medium for 3 hours. Stir well and season to taste with salt and pepper.
3. Use a vegetable peeler to cut the courgettes into long ribbons and lay them over the top in an even layer.
4. Mix the mozzarella with the cream and herbs and spoon the mixture over the top. Cover the slow cooker and cook for 1 hour.

Smart tip

Try browning the top of
the bake under the grill
just before serving.

Smart tip

Parboiling the potatoes gives them a head start and removes some of the starch.

Tartiflette

Preparation time
20 minutes

Cooking time
4 hours

Serves 4

Ingredients

800 g / 1 lb 12 oz / 2 ½ cups
    Maris Piper potatoes,
    peeled and sliced
salt
2 tbsp olive oil
1 onion, thinly sliced
150 g / 5 ½ oz / 1 cup
    smoked lardons
300 ml / 10 ½ fl. oz / 1 ¼ cups
    double (heavy) cream
200 ml / 7 fl. oz / ¾ cup
    vegetable stock
200 g / 7 oz / ¾ cup
    reblochon, sliced

Method

1. Parboil the potatoes in salted water for 6 minutes then drain well.
2. Meanwhile, heat the oil in a frying pan and fry the onion and lardons for 5 minutes.
3. Transfer the potatoes, onions and lardons to a slow cooker and stir in the cream and stock. Cover and cook on low for 4 hours or until the potatoes are tender.
4. Top the tartiflette with reblochon slices and finish the dish under a hot grill to toast the top.

Chicken and carrot pot pies

Preparation time
15 minutes

Cooking time
4 hours 25 minutes

Serves 6

Ingredients

2 tbsp butter
3 chicken breasts, cubed
2 tbsp plain (all-purpose) flour
salt and freshly ground
    black pepper
1 leek, finely chopped
2 carrots, chopped
300 ml / 10 ½ fl. oz / 1 ¼ cups
    chicken stock
300 ml / 10 ½ fl. oz / 1 ¼ cups
    double (heavy) cream
2 tbsp chives, chopped
300 g / 10 ½ oz / 1 ⅓
    all-butter puff pastry
1 egg, beaten

Method

1. Heat the butter in a frying pan. Dust the chicken pieces with flour and season with salt and pepper, then sear them all over.

2. Transfer the chicken to a slow cooker and mix with the rest of the ingredients, except for the chives, pastry and egg.

3. Cook on low for 4 hours, then taste the sauce for seasoning and adjust with salt and black pepper. Stir in the chives, then divide the mixture between six individual pie dishes.

4. Preheat the oven to 200°C (180°C fan) / 400F / gas 6. Roll out the pastry on a floured surface and cut out six lids. Brush the edges of the dishes with egg and lay the lids on top, then brush the tops with egg.

5. Bake the pies for 25 minutes or until the pastry is puffy and golden brown.

Smart tip

Use a fork to crimp the
edge of the pastry onto
the dish to seal.

Smart tip

Chicken stock can be used if you're unable to find lamb stock.

Lamb and pepper pasta bake

Preparation time
25 minutes

Cooking time
6 hours

Serves 4

Ingredients

450 g / 1 lb / 3 cups lamb
  shoulder, cubed
1 green pepper, sliced
1 onion, sliced
200 g / 7 oz / 1 cup canned
  tomatoes, chopped
200 ml / 7 fl. oz / ¾ cup white
  wine
400 ml / 14 fl. oz / 1 ½ cups
  lamb stock
1 tsp smoked paprika
1 bay leaf
400 g / 14 oz / 2 ½ cups dried
  fusilli pasta

For the topping:
2 tbsp butter
2 tbsp plain (all-purpose) flour
400 ml / 14 fl. oz / 1 ⅔ cups
  milk
75 g / 2 ½ oz / ¾ cup
  Parmesan, finely grated

Method

1. Mix the lamb, pepper, onion, tomatoes, wine, stock, paprika,
   bay leaf and pasta together in a slow cooker. Cover and cook
   on medium for 6 hours or until the lamb is tender and the
   pasta is al dente. Season to taste with salt and pepper.

2. To make the topping, melt the butter in a small saucepan.
   Stir in the flour then gradually incorporate the milk, stirring
   continuously to avoid any lumps forming.

3. When the mixture starts to bubble, stir in the cheese, then
   pour the sauce over the pasta. Brown the top under a hot grill
   and serve straight away.

Chicken and sage cannelloni

Preparation time
30 minutes

Cooking time
4 hours 30 minutes

Serves 4

Ingredients

3 tbsp olive oil
1 onion, finely chopped
4 cloves of garlic, crushed
450 g / 1 lb / 3 cups minced
    chicken
200 ml / 7 fl. oz / ¾ cup white
    wine
400 ml / 14 fl. oz / 1 ½ cups
    chicken stock
2 tbsp fresh sage leaves,
    finely chopped
75 g / 2 ½ oz / ¾ cup
    Parmesan, finely grated
12 fresh pasta sheets

Method

1. Heat the oil in a large frying pan and fry the onion and garlic for 5 minutes, stirring occasionally. Add the mince and fry until it starts to brown.

2. Pour in the wine and boil rapidly for 2 minutes, then scrape everything into a slow cooker with the stock and half of the sage.

3. Cover the slow cooker and cook on medium for 4 hours. Stir in the rest of the sage and half of the Parmesan, then season with salt and pepper to taste.

4. Preheat the oven to 200°C (180°C fan) / 390F / gas 6. Tip the chicken mixture into a sieve, reserving the cooking stock. Divide the filling between the pasta sheets, then roll them up and cut in half.

5. Arrange the cannelloni in a baking dish, then pour over the cooking stock and top with the rest of the Parmesan. Bake for 30 minutes or until golden brown.

Smart tip
You can also use dried
sage - reduce to 1 tsp
and add it all before
cooking.

Smart tip

Cut the lemon into quarters and serve with the chicken for squeezing over.

Coconut chicken

Preparation time
5 minutes

Cooking time
4 hours

Serves 4

Ingredients

4 chicken breasts, cubed
400 ml / 14 fl. oz / 1 ⅔ cups
    coconut milk
3 tbsp desiccated coconut
2 cloves of garlic,
    finely chopped
2.5 cm (1 in) piece ginger,
    finely chopped
½ tsp ground coriander
    (cilantro)
½ tsp ground cinnamon
1 tsp caster (superfine) sugar
1 lemon, zest finely grated
salt
coriander (cilantro) sprigs
    to garnish

Method

1. Put all of the ingredients except for the coriander sprigs in a slow cooker and stir well. Cover and cook on low for 4 hours, stirring halfway through.
2. Taste the sauce and add salt as necessary. Garnish with coriander sprigs before serving.

Vegetable lasagne

Preparation time
30 minutes

Cooking time
3 hours

Serves 4

Ingredients

1 onion, quartered
2 cloves of garlic, crushed
200 g / 7 oz / 2 ⅔ cups button
  mushrooms
16 tomatoes, halved
2 tbsp fresh thyme leaves
4 tbsp cream cheese
salt and freshly ground
  black pepper
8 sheets ready-made
  fresh pasta
2 tbsp plain (all-purpose) flour
4 tbsp fresh white
  breadcrumbs
4 tbsp Parmesan, finely grated
4 tbsp olive oil
basil leaves to garnish

Method

1. Put the onion, garlic and mushrooms in a food processor with half of the tomatoes, half the thyme and the cream cheese. Season with salt and pepper then pulse until finely chopped and evenly mixed.

2. Lay four of the pasta sheets in a line on the work surface with the long edges just overlapping. Top with half of the filling, then roll up and transfer to one side of a slow cooker. Repeat with the other four pasta sheets and lay the roll next to the first roll.

3. Top the pasta with the rest of the tomato halves and thyme. Mix the breadcrumbs and Parmesan together and sprinkle on top, then drizzle over the olive oil.

4. Cover the slow cooker and cook on medium for 3 hours or until a knife will slide easily into the centre. Garnish with fresh basil leaves and serve immediately.

Smart tip

The vegetables should let out enough liquid to cook the pasta, but if it starts to catch at any point, add a splash of water.

Smart tip

If you can't find Emmental, use another mild, melting cheese, to avoid overpowering the fish.

Fish pie

Preparation time
35 minutes

Cooking time
2 hours 30 minutes

Serves 4

Ingredients

450 g / 1 lb / 3 cups undyed
    smoked haddock fillet,
    cut into chunks
1 leek, finely chopped
2 cloves of garlic, crushed
300 ml / 10 ½ fl. oz / 1 ¼ cups
    fish stock
150 ml / 5 ½ fl. oz / ⅔ cup
    double (heavy) cream
225 g / 8 oz / 1 ½ cups brown
    shrimps, peeled
100 g / 3 ½ oz / 3 cups baby
    leaf spinach, washed
white pepper

For the topping:
900 g / 2 lb / 3 ½ cups Desiree
    potatoes, peeled
    and cubed
200 g / 7 oz / ¾ cup butter,
    cubed
100 ml / 3 ½ oz / ½ cup milk
salt and freshly ground
    black pepper
50 g / 1 ¾ oz / ½ cup
    Emmental, grated

Method

1. Mix the haddock, leek, garlic, stock and cream in a slow
   cooker. Put on the lid and cook on low for 2 hours.

2. Stir in the shrimps and spinach, then put the lid back on and
   cook for a further 30 minutes. Taste the sauce – it shouldn't
   need any salt, but might need a little white pepper.

3. To make the topping, cook the potatoes in boiling salted
   water for 12 minutes or until tender. Tip the potatoes into a
   colander and leave to drain.

4. Put the saucepan back on the heat, add the butter and
   milk and bring to a simmer. Use a potato ricer to crush the
   potatoes straight into the hot milk, then briefly beat the
   mixture with a wooden spoon until smooth. Season to taste
   with salt and pepper.

5. Spoon the potato on top of the haddock mixture and top
   with the Emmental, then lightly brown the top under a hot
   grill before serving.

Lamb and onions with potato gratin topping

Preparation time
35 minutes

Cooking time
6 hours

Serves 4

Ingredients

2 tbsp butter
3 onions, sliced
3 cloves of garlic, sliced
750 g / 1 lb 10 oz / 5 cups
 lamb shoulder, boned
700 ml / 1 pint 3 ½ fl. oz / 2 ¾
 cups dry white wine
salt and freshly ground
 black pepper

For the topping:
900 g / 2 lb / 3 ½ cups
 Desiree potatoes, peeled
 and cubed
200 g / 7 oz / ¾ cup butter,
 cubed
100 ml / 3 ½ oz / ½ cup milk
2 tbsp flat leaf parsley,
 chopped
salt and freshly ground
 black pepper
3 tbsp Parmesan, finely grated

Method

1. Heat the butter in a large sauté pan then fry the onions and garlic over a low heat for 15 minutes, stirring occasionally, until lightly caramelised.

2. Tip the onion mixture into a slow cooker and position the lamb on top, then pour over the wine.

3. Put the lid on the slow cooker and cook on low for 6 hours, then shred the meat apart with two forks. Stir well and season to taste with salt and pepper.

4. To make the topping, cook the potatoes in boiling salted water for 12 minutes or until tender. Tip the potatoes into a colander and leave to drain.

5. Put the saucepan back on the heat, add the butter and milk and bring to a simmer. Use a potato ricer to crush the potatoes straight into the hot milk, then briefly beat the mixture with a wooden spoon until smooth. Stir in the parsley and season to taste with salt and pepper.

6. Spoon the potato on top of the lamb and top with the Parmesan, then lightly brown the top under a hot grill before serving.

Smart tip

If the lamb won't shred after the cooking time, cook for a further hour and try again.

Smart tip

Cut the potatoes into even slices so that they all finish cooking at the same time.

Cheese, tomato and potato bake

Preparation time
15 minutes

Cooking time
4 hours

Serves 4

Ingredients

400 g / 14 oz / 2 cups canned
    tomatoes, chopped
2 cloves of garlic,
    finely chopped
1 tsp smoked paprika
salt and freshly ground
    black pepper
150 g / 5 ½ oz / 1 ½ cups
    Cheddar, grated
150 ml / 5 ½ fl. oz / ⅔ cup
    double (heavy) cream
600 g / 1 lb 5 ½ oz / 2 ½
    potatoes, peeled and sliced

Method

1. Mix the tomatoes with the garlic and paprika and season well
   with salt and pepper.
2. Stir the cheese into the cream. Layer up the potatoes with the
   tomato mixture and cheese mixture in a slow cooker.
3. Cover and cook on medium for 4 hours or until a skewer will
   slide in to the middle. Lightly brown the top under a hot grill
   before serving.

Chicken and leek pie

Preparation time
15 minutes

Cooking time
4 hours 30 minutes

Serves 6

Ingredients

3 chicken breasts, cubed
3 leeks, thickly sliced
300 ml / 10 ½ fl. oz / 1 ¼ cups
  chicken stock
300 ml / 10 ½ fl. oz / 1 ¼ cups
  double (heavy) cream
salt and freshly ground
  black pepper
300 g / 10 ½ oz / 1 ⅓ all-butter
  puff pastry
1 egg, beaten

Method

1. Mix the chicken and leeks with the stock and cream in a slow cooker.

2. Cover and cook on low for 4 hours, then taste the sauce for seasoning and adjust with salt and white pepper. Tip the mixture into a pie dish.

3. Preheat the oven to 200°C (180°C fan) / 400F / gas 6. Roll out the pastry on a floured surface. Brush the rim of the pie dish with egg, then lay the pastry on top and trim off any excess. Crimp around the edge with your thumb and finger to seal, then brush with beaten egg.

4. Bake the pie for 30 minutes or until the pastry is puffy and golden brown.

Smart tip

Try adding herbs of
your choice to the
creamy sauce.

Smart tip
Any leftover cooking stock can be used to make pea and ham soup.

Ham, potato and onion pie

Preparation time
30 minutes

Cooking time
6 hours 30 minutes

Serves 4

Ingredients

1 ham hock
450 g / 1 lb / 1 ¼ cups
   potatoes, peeled and sliced
2 tbsp butter
2 onions, sliced
1 clove of garlic, crushed
300 ml / 10 ½ fl. oz / 1 ¼ cups
   vegetable stock
225 g / 8 oz / ¾ cups
   all-butter puff pastry
1 egg, beaten

Method

1. Put the ham hock in a slow cooker and pour over enough water to cover by 2.5 cm (1 in). Cover and cook on medium for 6 hours, then shred the ham off the bone and reserve the cooking stock.

2. Preheat the oven to 200°C (180°C fan) / 400F / gas 6.

3. Parboil the potatoes in salted water for 10 minutes, then drain well.

4. Heat the butter in a large frying pan and fry the onions and garlic for 10 minutes to soften without browning. Stir in the ham and the cooking stock and bring to a simmer, then season to taste.

5. Stir in the potatoes and transfer the mixture to a baking dish.

6. Roll the pastry into a circle and lay it on top of the filling, then brush with beaten egg.

7. Bake the pie in the oven for 30 minutes or until the pastry is golden brown on top.

Lamb, aubergine and tomato bake

Preparation time
30 minutes

Cooking time
4 hours

Serves 4

Ingredients

2 tbsp butter
2 tbsp plain (all-purpose) flour
600 ml / 1 pint / 2 ½ cups milk
½ tsp nutmeg
salt and freshly ground
    black pepper
450 g / 1 lb / 3 cups lamb
    mince
2 shallots, chopped
2 cloves of garlic, crushed
½ tsp dried oregano
1 aubergine (eggplant), cubed
2 large tomatoes, cubed

Method

1. Melt the butter in a saucepan. Stir in the flour then gradually incorporate the milk, stirring continuously to avoid any lumps forming.

2. When the mixture starts to bubble, stir in the nutmeg and season to taste with salt and pepper.

3. Mix the lamb mince with the shallots, garlic, oregano, aubergine and tomatoes and season with salt and pepper.

4. Layer up the lamb mixture with the sauce inside a slow cooker, then cover and cook on medium for 4 hours.

Smart tip
Try sprinkling the
finished dish with
cheese and toasting it
under a hot grill.

Smart tip

Fresh cooking chorizo
can also be used, but
increase the quantity
to 350 g / 12 oz /
2 ⅓ cups.

Chorizo and squash pasta bake

Preparation time
5 minutes

Cooking time
4 hours

Serves 4

Ingredients

225 g / 8 oz / 1 ½ cups chorizo, diced

½ butternut squash, peeled and diced

200 g / 7 oz / 1 cup canned tomatoes, chopped

200 ml / 7 fl. oz / ¾ cup white wine

400 ml / 14 fl. oz / 1 ½ cups tomato passata

400 g / 14 oz / 2 ½ cups dried fusilli pasta

150 g / 5 ½ oz / ⅔ cup soft goats' cheese, crumbled

sage leaves to garnish

Method

1. Mix all of the ingredients, except for the cheese and sage, together in a slow cooker. Cover and cook on medium for 4 hours or until the pasta and squash are al dente. Season to taste with salt and pepper.

2. Top with the goats' cheese and sage leaves before serving.

Ham and mushroom cannelloni

Preparation time
45 minutes

Cooking time
2 hours

Serves 4

Ingredients

50 g / 1 ¾ oz / ¼ cup butter
2 shallots, chopped
2 cloves of garlic, crushed
200 g / 7 oz / 2 ⅔ cups button
    mushrooms, chopped
12 sheets ready-made
    fresh pasta
2 tbsp plain (all-purpose) flour
600 ml / 1 pint / 2 ½ cups milk
200 g / 7 oz / 2 cups
    Emmental, grated
150 g / 5 ½ oz / 1 cup cooked
    ham, in small cubes
1 tbsp basil leaves, chopped
salt and freshly ground
    black pepper

Method

1. Melt half the butter in a frying pan and fry the shallots and garlic for 5 minutes. Add the mushrooms with a pinch of salt and cook for another 5 minutes.

2. Meanwhile, melt the rest of the butter in a small saucepan. Stir in the flour then gradually incorporate the milk, stirring continuously to avoid any lumps forming.

3. When the mixture starts to bubble, stir in half the cheese, the ham, basil and a grind of black pepper, then take the pan off the heat.

4. Add half of the sauce to the mushroom mixture and stir.

5. Split the mushroom filling between the pasta sheets, then roll them up and pack them into a slow cooker.

6. Pour over the rest of the sauce and sprinkle with the other half of the cheese. Cook on low for 2 hours, then brown the top under a hot grill before serving.

Smart tip

If you can't find fresh
pasta sheets, parboil
dried lasagne for
4 minutes.

Smart tip

Removing the excess liquid from the filling stops the pie from having a soggy bottom.

Spinach, bacon and mushroom pie

Preparation time
15 minutes

Cooking time
3 hours 40 minutes

Serves 6

Ingredients

200 g / 7 oz / 8 cups spinach, washed and chopped
300 g / 10 ½ oz / 4 cups mushrooms, chopped
100 g / 2 ⅓ oz / ½ cup lardons
1 leek, finely chopped
2 cloves of garlic, crushed
2 tbsp butter, diced
250 ml / 7 fl. oz / 1 cup ham stock
salt and freshly ground black pepper
450 g / 1 lb / 1 ½ cups all-butter puff pastry
1 egg, beaten

Method

1. Mix the spinach, mushrooms, lardons, leek, garlic, butter and stock together in a slow cooker.

2. Cover the slow cooker and cook on medium for 3 hours, then tip the mixture into a colander to remove any excess liquid. Season to taste with salt and pepper.

3. Preheat the oven to 200°C (180°C fan) / 400F / gas 6.

4. Roll out half the pastry on a floured surface and use it to line a pie tin. Spoon in the spinach mixture, then roll out the rest of the pastry and lay it on top.

5. Fold over the edges to enclose and brush the top with egg, then bake for 40 minutes or until the pastry is cooked through underneath and golden brown on top.

Ham and chicory bake

Preparation time
20 minutes

Cooking time
3 hours

Serves 4

Ingredients

2 tbsp butter
2 tbsp plain (all-purpose) flour
600 ml / 1 pint / 2 ½ cups milk
1 tbsp Dijon mustard
150 g / 5 ½ oz / 1 ½ cups
    Cheddar, grated
4 heads of chicory
4 slices of ham

Method

1. Melt the butter in a medium saucepan then stir in the flour. Gradually whisk in the milk a little at a time until it is all incorporated, then stir in the mustard and half of the cheese.

2. Wrap each chicory head in a slice of ham and arrange in a single layer in a small slow cooker. Pour over the sauce and cook on medium for 3 hours or until a skewer will slide easily into the chicory.

3. Sprinkle the rest of the cheese on top and brown it slightly under a hot grill before serving.

Smart tip

There's no need to thicken the sauce in the pan as it will thicken in the slow cooker.

Smart tip

Dress the top with a little olive oil before serving.

Tomato and aubergine parmigiana

Preparation time
10 minutes

Cooking time
4 hours

Serves 4

Ingredients

4 large ripe tomatoes,
   chopped
2 cloves of garlic,
   fincly chopped
1 tbsp fresh thyme leaves
salt and freshly ground
   black pepper
2 aubergines (eggplants),
   sliced
2 mozzarella balls, sliced

Method

1. Toss the tomatoes with the garlic and thyme and season
   with salt and pepper. Layer up the tomato mixture with the
   aubergine and mozzarella slices in a small slow cooker.

2. Cover and cook on medium for 4 hours. Lightly brown the
   top under a hot grill before serving.

Sausage and tomato pasta bake

Preparation time
20 minutes

Cooking time
3 hours

Serves 4

Ingredients

450 g / 1 lb / 2 cups sausages, cut into chunks
150 g / 5 ½ oz / 2 cups button mushrooms, sliced
225 g / 8 oz / 1 ½ cups cherry tomatoes, halved
200 g / 7 oz / 1 cup canned sweetcorn, drained
200 ml / 7 fl. oz / ¾ cup white wine
400 ml / 14 fl. oz / 1 ½ cups chicken stock
400 g / 14 oz / 2 ½ cups dried rigatoni pasta
50 g / 1 ¾ oz / ½ cup Gruyère cheese, grated
basil leaves to garnish

Method

1. Mix all of the ingredients, except for the cheese and basil, together in a slow cooker. Cover and cook on medium for 3 hours or until the pasta is al dente. Season to taste with salt and pepper.

2. Sprinkle the top with cheese, then melt it under a hot grill. Garnish with basil before serving.

Smart tip

Stir the pasta every
hour to help it
cook evenly.

Smart tip

Look out for aged Gruyère for a greater strength of cheese.

Cauliflower cheese with ham

Preparation time
15 minutes

Cooking time
3 hours

Serves 4

Ingredients

1 cauliflower, cut into florets
2 tbsp butter
2 tbsp plain (all-purpose) flour
600 ml / 1 pint / 2 ½ cups milk
1 tbsp Dijon mustard
3 slices cooked ham, chopped
75 g / 2 ½ oz / ¾ cup Gruyère,
   grated

Method

1. Arrange the cauliflower florets in a slow cooker.
2. Melt the butter in a medium saucepan then stir in the flour. Gradually whisk in the milk a little at a time until it is all incorporated, then stir in the mustard, ham and cheese.
3. Pour the sauce over the cauliflower, then cover the slow cooker and cook on medium for 3 hours, or until the cauliflower is cooked al dente.
4. Brown the top under a hot grill before serving.

Italian sausage meat pie

Preparation time
25 minutes

Cooking time
3 hours 40 minutes

Serves 6

Ingredients

250 g / 9 oz / 1 ⅔ cups
    coarsely minced pork
250 g / 9 oz / 1 ⅔ cups
    sausage meat
1 red onion, grated
2 cloves of garlic, crushed
1 tsp fennel seeds, crushed
1 tbsp concentrated
    tomato purée
salt and white pepper
125 ml / 4 fl. oz / ½ cup
    chicken stock
450 g / 1 lb / 1 ½ cups
    all-butter puff pastry
1 egg, beaten

Method

1. Mix the pork, sausage meat, onion, garlic, fennel seeds, tomato purée and stock together in a slow cooker and season with salt and plenty of white pepper.

2. Cover the slow cooker and cook on medium for 3 hours, then tip the mixture into a sieve to remove any excess liquid. Season to taste with salt and pepper.

3. Preheat the oven to 200°C (180°C fan) / 400F / gas 6.

4. Roll out half the pastry on a floured surface and use it to line a pie tin. Spoon in the sausage meat mixture, then roll out the rest of the pastry and lay it on top.

5. Fold over the edges to enclose and brush the top with egg, then bake for 40 minutes or until the pastry is cooked through underneath and golden brown on top.

Smart tip
This pie is also delicious spiced with 1 tsp of dried chilli (chili) flakes.

Smart tip

Adding rice to the lamb
helps to absorb excess
moisture that would
otherwise make the
crumble soggy.

Lamb and vegetable crumble

Preparation time
25 minutes

Cooking time
4 hours 30 minutes

Serves 6

Ingredients

2 tbsp olive oil
800 g / 1 lb 12 oz / 5 cups
    lamb shoulder, cubed
1 leek, finely chopped
2 carrots, julienned
2 courgettes (zucchinis), sliced
100 g / 3 ½ oz / ½ cup long
    grain rice
600 ml / 1 pint / 2 ½ cups
    lamb stock
salt and freshly ground
    black pepper

For the crumble:

75 g / 2 ½ oz / ⅓ cup butter
50 g / 1 ¾ oz / ⅓ cup plain
    (all-purpose) flour
25 g / 1 oz / ¼ cup ground
    almonds
50 g / 1 ¾ oz / ½ cup porridge
    oats
3 tbsp Parmesan, finely grated

Method

1. Heat the oil in a frying pan, then sear the lamb on all
   sides. Transfer the lamb to a slow cooker and mix with the
   vegetables, rice and stock.

2. Cook on medium for 4 hours, then taste the sauce for
   seasoning and adjust with salt and black pepper.

3. Preheat the oven to 180°C (160°C fan) / 350F / gas 4. Rub the
   butter into the flour until it resembles breadcrumbs, then stir
   in the almonds, oats and Parmesan.

4. Tip the lamb mixture into a baking dish and top with the
   crumble. Bake the crumble for 30 minutes or until the topping
   is golden brown.

Chicken and aubergine bake

Preparation time
10 minutes

Cooking time
4 hours

Serves 4

Ingredients

4 boned chicken thighs,
    skinned and cubed
2 cloves of garlic,
    finely chopped
1 tbsp fresh thyme leaves
salt and freshly ground
    black pepper
2 aubergines (eggplants),
    sliced
2 mozzarella balls, sliced
250 ml / 9 fl. oz / 1 cup chicken
    stock

Method

1. Toss the chicken with the garlic and thyme and season with salt and pepper. Layer up the chicken mixture with the aubergine and mozzarella slices in a small slow cooker, then pour over the stock.

2. Cover and cook on medium for 4 hours. Lightly brown the top under a hot grill before serving.

Smart tip

Insert a skewer into the centre to test if the bake is ready to eat.

Cakes and Sweet Bakes

Baked apples

Preparation time
30 minutes

Cooking time
3 hours

Serves 8

Ingredients

8 dessert apples
75 g / 2 ½ oz / ⅔ cup walnuts, chopped
100 g / 3 ½ oz / ½ cup dried figs, chopped
2 tbsp butter, softened
3 tbsp runny honey
250 ml / 9 fl. oz / 1 cup apple juice

Method

1. Use a sharp paring knife to remove the apple cores, then cut off and reserve the tops.
2. Mix the walnuts with the figs, butter and honey, then pack the mixture into the apple cavities and replace the tops.
3. Pack the apples into a slow cooker in a single layer, then pour the apple juice around.
4. Cover and cook on medium for 3 hours or until the apples are tender to the point of a knife.

Smart tip

Check the apples once an hour and if the juice has almost evaporated, top up with water.

Smart tip
Slow cooking the clafoutis gives them a deliciously velvety texture.

Cherry clafoutis

Preparation time
25 minutes

Cooking time
3 hours

Makes 8

Ingredients

75 g / 2 ½ oz / ⅓ cup butter
75 g / 2 ½ oz / ⅓ cup caster
  (superfine) sugar
300 ml / 10 ½ fl. oz / 1 ¼ cups
  whole milk
2 large eggs
50 g / 1 ¾ oz / ⅓ cup plain
  (all-purpose) flour
pinch of salt
2 tbsp ground almonds
300 g / 10 ½ oz / 2 cups
  cherries, stoned
4 tbsp flaked (slivered)
  almonds
icing (confectioners') sugar
  for dusting

Method

1. Melt the butter in a saucepan and cook over a low heat until
   it starts to smell nutty. Brush a little of the butter around the
   inside of eight ramekins then sprinkle with caster sugar and
   shake to coat.

2. Whisk together the milk and eggs with the rest of the butter.
   Sift the flour into a mixing bowl with a pinch of salt, then stir in
   the ground almonds and the rest of the sugar.

3. Make a well in the middle of the dry ingredients and gradually
   whisk in the liquid, incorporating all the flour from round the
   outside until you have a lump-free batter.

4. Arrange the cherries in the prepared ramekins, then pour in
   the batter and scatter with flaked almonds.

5. Cover each ramekin with a square of buttered foil and
   arrange them in a slow cooker. Add enough boiling water to
   come halfway up the sides, then cover and cook on low for
   3 hours or until the clafoutis are set with just a slight wobble
   in the centres.

6. Toast the tops of the clafoutis under a hot grill, then serve
   sprinkled with icing sugar.

Vanilla cheesecake

Preparation time
30 minutes

Cooking time
3 hours

Chilling time
2 hours

Serves 8

Ingredients

200 g / 7 oz / 2 cups digestive
  biscuits, crushed
50 g / 1 ¾ oz / ¼ cup butter,
  melted
600 g / 1 lb 5 oz / 2 ¾ cups
  cream cheese
150 ml / 5 fl. oz / ⅔ cup soured
  cream
2 large eggs, plus 1 egg yolk
1 vanilla pod, seeds only
2 tbsp plain (all-purpose) flour
100 ml / 3 ½ fl. oz / ⅓ cup
  runny honey
75 g / 2 ½ oz / ⅓ cup caster
  (superfine) sugar

Method

1. Mix the biscuit crumbs with the butter and press into an even
   layer in the bottom of a spring-form cake tin that will fit inside
   your slow cooker.

2. Whisk together the rest of the ingredients until smooth, then
   pour the mixture into the tin and level the surface.

3. Put a rack into the bottom of your slow cooker and add 2.5 cm
   (1 in) of boiling water, then position the cake tin on top. Cover
   the top of the slow cooker with 3 layers of kitchen paper
   before putting on the lid.

4. Cook on high for 2 hours, then turn off the slow cooker and
   leave to cook in the residual heat without lifting the lid for
   1 hour.

5. Take the cheesecake out of the slow cooker and leave to cool
   to room temperature before chilling for at least 2 hours.

Smart tip

The kitchen paper will collect the condensed steam and stop it from dripping onto the cheesecake.

Smart tip

These desserts are also delicious made in advance and served chilled.

Rice pudding with apple and caramel compote

Preparation time
10 minutes

Cooking time
5 hours

Serves 6

Ingredients

50 g / 1 ¾ oz / ¼ cup butter, plus extra for buttering
1.2 litres / 2 pints / 4 ½ cups whole milk
1 vanilla pod, halved lengthways
110 g / 4 oz / ½ cup short grain rice
75 g / 2 ½ oz / ⅓ cup caster (superfine) sugar

For the compote:
1 bramley apple, peeled, cored and diced
4 eating apples, peeled, cored and diced
½ lemon, juiced
4 tbsp apple juice
4 tbsp caramel sauce

Method

1. Butter the inside of a slow cooker. Stir all of the rice pudding ingredients together, then tip the mixture into the slow cooker.

2. Cook on high for 3 hours, stirring once every hour. Scrape the rice pudding into a container, then wash and dry the slow cooker.

3. To make the compote, put the apples, lemon juice and apple juice in the slow cooker, then cover and cook on high for 2 hours. Stir in the caramel sauce.

4. Spoon the apple compote into six heatproof glasses and top with the rice pudding. Toast the top under a hot grill before serving.

Lemon yoghurt cake

Preparation time
45 minutes

Cooking time
3 hours

Serves 8

Ingredients

125 ml / 4 ½ fl. oz / ½ cup
  sunflower oil
200 g / 7 oz / 1 cup caster
  (superfine) sugar
1 lemon, juiced and zest
  finely grated
3 large eggs
125 ml / 4 ½ fl. oz / ½ cup
  natural yoghurt
150 g / 5 ½ oz / 1 cup
  self-raising flour

To serve:
300 g / 10 ½ oz / 2 cups mixed
  summer berries
3 tbsp icing (confectioners')
  sugar, plus extra for dusting
2 ripe peaches, peeled,
  stoned and sliced

Method

1. Put a rack in the bottom of a slow cooker and add 2.5 cm
   (1 in) of boiling water. Butter a deep, round cake tin that will fit
   inside your slow cooker.

2. Measure the oil, sugar, lemon juice and zest, eggs and
   yoghurt into a mixing bowl and whisk together until smoothly
   combined. Fold in the flour.

3. Scrape the mixture into the tin then transfer it to the slow
   cooker. Cook on high for 3 hours or until a skewer inserted in
   the centre comes out clean. Transfer the cake to a wire rack
   and leave to cool completely.

4. Put half of the berries in a liquidiser with the icing sugar and
   blend until smooth. Pass the sauce through a sieve to remove
   the seeds.

5. When the cake has cooled, cut it into slices and top with the
   peaches, a drizzle of sauce and the rest of the berries. Dust
   with a little icing sugar and serve immediately.

Smart tip

Sieve the flour before folding in for an extra light cake.

Smart tip

If you're not able to
find dulce de leche,
replace it with caramel
sauce or honey.

Rice pudding with dulce de leche and pistachios

Preparation time
10 minutes

Cooking time
3 hours

Serves 4

Ingredients

110 g / 4 oz / ½ cup short
   grain rice
1.2 litres / 2 pints / 4 ½ cups
   whole milk
75 g / 2 ½ oz / ¼ cup dulce de
   leche, plus extra to serve
50 g / 1 ¾ oz / ¼ cup butter
   diced, plus extra for
   buttering
½ tsp almond extract
2 tbsp pistachio nuts, chopped

Method

1. Butter the inside of a slow cooker. Stir the rice, milk, dulce
   de leche, butter and almond extract together and pour the
   mixture into the slow cooker.

2. Cook on high for 3 hours, stirring once every hour.

3. Serve hot or chilled with extra dulce de leche drizzled over
   and a sprinkle of pistachios.

Yoghurt panna cotta with sharon fruit compote

Preparation time
1 hour

Cooking time
1 hour 30 minutes

Chilling time
4 hours

Serves 6

Ingredients

300 ml / 10 ½ fl. oz / 1 ¼ cups
   double (heavy) cream
4 tbsp runny honey
3 sheets leaf gelatine
4 tbsp milk
300 ml / 10 ½ fl. oz / 1 ¼ cups
   Greek yoghurt

For the compote:
12 sharon fruit, peeled
   and chopped
1 lemon, juiced
4 tbsp caster (superfine) sugar

For the cocoa cream:
150 ml / 5 ½ fl. oz / ⅔ cup
   double (heavy) cream
1 tbsp unsweetened
   cocoa powder
1 tbsp runny honey

Method

1. First make the panna cotta. Heat the cream with the honey until small bubbles appear at the edges of the pan. Take the pan off the heat and leave to cool a little.

2. Break up the gelatine sheets and put them in a shallow dish. Pour over the milk and leave to soften for 10 minutes, then whisk the mixture into the warm cream.

3. When the gelatine has fully dissolved, strain the cream into a jug and leave to cool. When the gelatine mixture starts to gel, fold in the yoghurt and divide between 6 small glasses.

4. Refrigerate for 4 hours or until set.

5. Meanwhile, toss the sharon fruit with the lemon juice and sugar in a slow cooker. Put on the lid and cook on low for 1 hour 30 minutes or until the fruit has started to break down. Blend to a smooth purée with a stick blender.

6. To make the cocoa cream, heat the cream in a small saucepan until it starts to simmer. Put the cocoa in a bowl, then whisk in the hot cream, followed by the honey. Leave to cool to room temperature, then chill until ready to use.

7. Spoon the sharon fruit compote on top of the panna cottas, then top with a little cocoa cream.

Smart tip

Sit the jug with the panna cotta mixture in a bowl of iced water to speed the cooling process.

Smart tip

If you can't find
pear liqueur, use
brandy instead.

Poached pears with chocolate and cinnamon

Preparation time
25 minutes

Cooking time
2 hours

Serves 6

Ingredients

3 tbsp caster (superfine) sugar
500 ml / 17 ½ fl. oz / 2 cups
    perry (pear cider)
6 pears, peeled and cored
200 g / 7 oz / 1 ¼ cups dark
    chocolate (minimum 60%
    cocoa solids)
150 ml / 5 ½ fl. oz / ⅔ cup
    double (heavy) cream
2 tbsp pear liqueur
1 tsp ground cinnamon
12 spiced biscuits

Method

1. Stir the sugar into the perry in a small slow cooker to dissolve, then add the pears and cover with a crumpled piece of greaseproof paper.

2. Cover and cook on medium for 2 hours, turning the pears halfway through. Leave in the cooking liquid to cool to room temperature.

3. Chop the chocolate and transfer it to a small saucepan with the cream and liqueur. Stir over a gentle heat until the chocolate melts and the sauce is smooth and shiny.

4. Remove the pears from the poaching liquid and leave to dry on a wire rack for 10 minutes. Transfer the pears to warm serving plates, then coat each one in the chocolate sauce. Sprinkle a little cinnamon over each one and serve with the spiced biscuits.

Camomile custards

Preparation time
20 minutes

Cooking time
3 hours

Chilling time
4 hours

Serves 6

Ingredients

600 ml / 1 pint / 2 ½ cups
    whole milk
2 tbsp dried camomile flowers
4 large eggs
2 tbsp caster (superfine) sugar

Method

1. Preheat the slow cooker to low.

2. Put the milk in a small saucepan with the camomile flowers and bring slowly to a simmer. Turn off the heat, cover the pan and leave to infuse for 10 minutes.

3. Whisk the eggs and sugar together, then strain the milk in through a sieve, stirring all the time. Pour the custard into 6 small pots or ramekins and cover the tops with foil.

4. Sit the pots in the slow cooker and pour enough boiling water around them to come halfway up the sides.

5. Cook on low for 3 hours or until the custards are just set with a slight wobble in the centre. Remove the pots from the slow cooker and chill for 4 hours or overnight before serving.

Smart tip

If you can't find dried
camomile flowers, use a
camomile tea
bag instead.

Smart tip

Make sure the bowl and whisk for the egg whites are completely grease-free before using.

Chocolate soufflés

Preparation time
20 minutes

Cooking time
1 hour

Serves 4

Ingredients

1 tbsp butter
3 tbsp caster (superfine) sugar
2 large egg whites
1 tbsp cornflour (cornstarch)
100 g / 3 ½ oz / ½ cup
   chocolate spread

Method

1. Put a rack inside a slow cooker and add 2.5 cm (1 in) of boiling water, then set it to high.

2. Butter four ramekins and use 1 tbsp of the sugar to coat the insides.

3. Whisk the egg whites with an electric whisk until stiff, then whisk in the rest of the sugar. Stir the cornflour into the chocolate spread, then fold in the egg whites.

4. Spoon the mixture into the prepared ramekins, then transfer them to the slow cooker. Lay 3 layers of kitchen paper over the top of the slow cooker before putting on the lid to absorb the condensed steam.

5. Cook for 1 hour or until the soufflés are only just set in the centres. Serve immediately.

Egg custards

Preparation time
20 minutes

Cooking time
3 hours

Chilling time
4 hours

Serves 6

Ingredients

600 ml / 1 pint / 2 ½ cups
   whole milk
6 large egg yolks
2 tbsp caster (superfine) sugar

Method

1. Preheat the slow cooker to low.

2. Put the milk in a small saucepan and bring slowly to a simmer.

3. Whisk the egg yolks and sugar together, then whisk in the hot milk. Pour the custard into 6 ramekins or bowls and cover the tops with foil.

4. Pour 2.5 cm (1 in) of water into the slow cooker, then arrange the ramekins in layers on racks.

5. Cook on low for 3 hours or until the custards are just set with a slight wobble in the centre. Remove the ramekins from the slow cooker and chill for 4 hours or overnight before serving.

Smart tip

Save the egg whites
and use them to
make a pavlova.

Smart tip

This is a great cake to serve coeliacs or people with gluten intolerance.

Orange and almond cake

Preparation time
15 minutes

Cooking time
3 hours

Serves 8

Ingredients

200 g / 7 oz / ¾ cup butter,
  softened
200 g / 7 oz / ¾ cup caster
  (superfine) sugar
3 large eggs
2 oranges, juiced and zest
  finely grated
125 g / 4 ½ oz / ¾ cup
  quick-cook polenta
250 g/ 9 oz / 2 ½ cups ground
  almonds
50 g / 1 ¾ oz / ⅓ cup cornflour
  (cornstarch)
2 tsp baking powder

Method

1. Put a rack in the bottom of a slow cooker and add 2.5 cm
   (1 in) of boiling water. Butter a deep, round cake tin that will
   fit inside your slow cooker.

2. Cream the butter and sugar together until smooth and pale.
   Lightly beat the eggs with the orange zest, then gradually
   beat them into the butter and sugar mixture. Mix the polenta
   with the ground almonds, cornflour and baking powder, then
   add it slowly to the mix, stopping as soon as everything is
   smoothly combined.

3. Scrape the mixture into the tin and level the top with a
   spatula, then transfer it to the slow cooker. Cook on high for
   3 hours or until a skewer inserted in the centre comes out
   clean. Transfer the cake to a wire rack and leave to
   cool completely.

Poached nectarines with redcurrants

Preparation time
30 minutes

Cooking time
1 hour 30 minutes

Serves 8

Ingredients

4 white-fleshed nectarines,
  halved and stoned
100 g / 3 ½ oz / ½ cup caster
  (superfine) sugar
300 g / 10 ½ oz / 2 cups
  redcurrant sprigs

Method

1. Put the nectarines in a slow cooker with the sugar and half the redcurrants and pour over 200 ml / 7 fl. oz / ¾ cup of water.

2. Cover and cook on medium for 1 hour 30 minutes or until the fruit is tender, but still holding its shape.

3. Peel off and discard the skins of the nectarines and divide between eight small bowls. Pass the cooking liquid through a fine sieve and spoon it over, then garnish with the rest of the redcurrant sprigs.

Smart tip

This recipe can be made with frozen redcurrants when fresh are not in season.

Smart tip
The unused egg whites can be stored in the fridge for up to 4 days.

Apricot and orange compote custards

Preparation time
45 minutes

Cooking time
5 hours

Chilling time
4 hours

Serves 8

Ingredients

16 apricots, peeled, stoned
  and chopped
1 orange, juiced and zest
  finely grated
4 tbsp caster (superfine) sugar

For the custard:
600 ml / 1 pint / 2 ½ cups
  whole milk
1 orange, zest cut into
  thin strips
4 large egg yolks
2 tbsp caster (superfine) sugar

Method

1. Put the apricots, orange juice, orange zest and sugar in a slow cooker and stir well.

2. Cover and cook on medium for 2 hours. Taste for sweetness and add extra sugar if necessary. Use a stick blender to purée the fruit, then half-fill 8 ramekins and leave to cool a little. Wash up the slow cooker.

3. Put the milk in a small saucepan with the orange zest and bring slowly to a simmer. Turn off the heat, cover the pan and leave to infuse for 10 minutes.

4. Whisk the egg yolks and sugar together, then strain the milk in through a sieve, stirring all the time. Top up the ramekins with the custard mixture and cover the tops with foil.

5. Sit the ramekins in the slow cooker and pour enough boiling water around them to come halfway up the sides.

6. Cook on low for 3 hours or until the custards are just set with a slight wobble in the centre. Remove the ramekins from the slow cooker and chill for 4 hours or overnight before serving.

Condensed milk sponge cake

Preparation time
45 minutes

Cooking time
3 hours

Serves 6

Ingredients

125 g / 4 ½ oz / ¾ cup
self-raising flour
85 g / 3 oz / ⅓ cup butter,
softened
250 g / 9 fl. oz / ¾ cup
condensed milk
1 large egg
½ tsp vanilla extract

To serve:
250 ml / 9 fl. oz / 1 cup double
(heavy) cream
100 ml / 3 ½ fl. oz / ½ cup
condensed milk
150 g / 5 ½ oz / 1 cup mixed
summer berries
3 tbsp strawberry sauce

Method

1. Put a rack in the bottom of a slow cooker and add 2.5 cm
   (1 in) of boiling water. Oil a loaf tin that will fit inside your slow
   cooker and line with greaseproof paper.

2. Whisk all of the cake ingredients together in a bowl until
   smooth. Scrape the mixture into the tin then transfer it to the
   slow cooker.

3. Cook on high for 3 hours or until a skewer inserted in the
   centre comes out clean. Transfer the cake to a wire rack and
   leave to cool completely.

4. Whip the cream until it holds its shape, then spoon it in a
   line down the centre of the cake. Drizzle with half of the
   condensed milk, then arrange half of the berries on top.

5. To serve, cut the cake into thick slices and transfer to plates
   that have been decorated with strawberry sauce and the rest
   of the condensed milk and berries.

Smart tip

Try replacing the strawberry sauce with a spoonful of fruity jam.

Smart tip
For a richer taste, infuse whole cinnamon sticks in the milk before adding the chocolate.

Chocolate and cinnamon custards

Preparation time
20 minutes

Cooking time
3 hours

Chilling time
4 hours

Serves 6

Ingredients

600 ml / 1 pint / 2 ½ cups
    whole milk
150 g / 5 ½ oz / ¾ cup dark
    chocolate (minimum 60 %
    cocoa solids), grated
6 large egg yolks
2 tbsp caster (superfine) sugar
½ tsp ground cinnamon

Method

1. Preheat the slow cooker to low.

2. Put the milk in a small saucepan and bring slowly to a simmer. Take the pan off the heat and leave to cool for 5 minutes, then stir in the grated chocolate.

3. Whisk the egg yolks, sugar and cinnamon together, then whisk in the warm milk. Pour the custard into 6 small pots or ramekins and cover the tops with foil.

4. Sit the pots in the slow cooker and pour enough boiling water around them to come halfway up the sides.

5. Cook on low for 3 hours or until the custards are just set with a slight wobble in the centre. Remove the pots from the slow cooker and chill for 4 hours or overnight before serving.

Vanilla poached cherries

Preparation time
10 minutes

Cooking time
1 hour 30 minutes

Serves 6

Ingredients

900 g / 2 lb / 5 cups black
  cherries, stoned
100 g / 3 ½ oz / ½ cup caster
  (superfine) sugar
100 ml / 3 ½ fl. oz / ½ cup rosé
  wine
1 vanilla pod, split lengthways
3 tbsp kirsch
vanilla ice cream to serve

Method

1. Mix the cherries with the sugar, wine and vanilla pod in a slow
   cooker. Cover and cook on medium for 1 hour 30 minutes
   then stir in the kirsch and leave to cool.
2. Discard the vanilla pod, then spoon the cherries and their
   cooking liquid into bowls and serve with vanilla ice cream.

Smart tip

Wash and dry the
vanilla pod, then store
it in your sugar jar for
vanilla-infused sugar.

Smart tip
You can store the compote in the fridge for up to a week.

Pear and apricot compote

Preparation time
15 minutes

Cooking time
2 hours 30 minutes

Serves 6

Ingredients

6 pears, peeled, cored
and chopped
6 apricots, peeled, stoned
and chopped
100 g / 3 ½ oz / ½ cup caster
(superfine) sugar
1 vanilla pod, halved
lengthways
1 lemon, juiced
yoghurt or fromage frais
to serve

Method

1. Put the pears, apricots, sugar and vanilla pod in a slow cooker
with a splash of water.

2. Cover and cook on medium for 2 hours 30 minutes or until
the fruit is tender.

3. Stir in the lemon juice, then store in a large kilner jar. Serve
with yoghurt or fromage frais, garnished with pieces of the
vanilla pod.

Strawberry compote with yoghurt cream

Preparation time
30 minutes

Cooking time
1 hour 30 minutes

Serves 6

Ingredients

225 g / 8 oz / 1 ½ cups
   strawberries, halved
100 g / 3 ½ oz / ½ cup caster
   (superfine) sugar
½ lemon, juiced
300 ml / 10 ½ fl. oz / 1 ¼ cups
   double (heavy) cream
4 tbsp runny honey
300 ml / 10 ½ fl. oz / 1 ¼ cups
   Greek yoghurt
2 tbsp toasted flaked (slivered)
   almonds

Method

1. Put the strawberries, sugar and lemon juice in a slow cooker. Cover and cook on low for 1 hour 30 minutes.

2. Transfer half of the strawberries to a bowl with a slotted spoon. Tip the rest of the strawberries and their cooking stock into a liquidiser and blend to a smooth sauce. Leave to cool to room temperature.

3. Whip the cream with the honey until it holds its shape, then fold in the yoghurt. Swirl the cream mixture onto a shallow serving bowl. Top with the strawberries and strawberry sauce, then sprinkle with toasted almonds. Serve immediately.

Smart tip

If you can't find toasted
almonds, toast your
own in a dry frying pan
for a few minutes.

Smart tip
Cooking the butter first gives a toasty hazelnut (cobnut) taste to the dish.

Apple and lemon clafoutis

Preparation time
25 minutes

Cooking time
3 hours

Makes 4

Ingredients

75 g / 2 ½ oz / ⅓ cup butter
75 g / 2 ½ oz / ⅓ cup caster
    (superfine) sugar
300 ml / 10 ½ fl. oz / 1 ¼ cups
    whole milk
2 large eggs
50 g / 1 ¾ oz / ⅓ cup plain
    (all-purpose) flour
pinch of salt
1 lemon, zest finely grated
2 tbsp ground almonds
2 dessert apples, peeled,
    cored and sliced
icing (confectioners') sugar
    for dusting

Method

1. Melt the butter in a saucepan and cook over a low heat until it starts to smell nutty. Brush a little of the butter around the inside of four individual gratin dishes then sprinkle with caster sugar and shake to coat.

2. Whisk together the milk and eggs with the rest of the butter. Sift the flour into a mixing bowl with a pinch of salt, then stir in the lemon zest, ground almonds and the rest of the sugar.

3. Make a well in the middle of the dry ingredients and gradually whisk in the liquid, incorporating all the flour from round the outside until you have a lump-free batter.

4. Arrange the apple slices in the prepared dishes, then pour in the batter.

5. Cover each dish with a square of buttered foil and arrange them in a slow cooker. Add enough boiling water to come halfway up the sides, then cover and cook on low for 3 hours, or until the clafoutis are set with a slight wobble in the centre.

6. Toast the tops of the clafoutis under a hot grill, then serve sprinkled with icing sugar.

Steamed lemon puddings

Preparation time
30 minutes

Cooking time
2 hours

Makes 8

Ingredients

200 g / 7 oz / 1 ⅓ cups
  self-raising flour
200 g / 7 oz / ¾ cup caster
  (superfine) sugar
200 g / 7 oz / ¾ cup butter,
  softened
4 large eggs
1 tsp baking powder
1 lemon, zest finely grated
8 tbsp lemon curd

Method

1. Butter eight individual pudding basins and put a slow cooker on high to preheat.
2. Put all of the ingredients except the lemon curd in a large mixing bowl and whisk with an electric whisk for 4 minutes.
3. Put a tablespoon of lemon curd into the bottom of each pudding basin, then divide the cake mixture between them.
4. Cover each basin with a square of buttered foil then transfer them to the slow cooker. Pour enough boiling water around them to come halfway up the sides, then cover and cook on high for 2 hours.
5. When the puddings are ready, a skewer inserted into the centre should come out clean. Turn the puddings out onto plates and serve warm.

Smart tip

Make sure you can fit all of the pudding basins in a single layer in your slow cooker.

Caramelised rice puddings

Preparation time
20 minutes

Cooking time
3 hours

Makes 6

Ingredients

50 g / 1 ¾ oz / ¼ cup butter,
plus extra for buttering
3 tbsp dark brown sugar
1.2 litres / 2 pints / 4 ½ cups
whole milk
1 tsp vanilla extract
110 g / 4 oz / ½ cup short
grain rice
75 g / 2 ½ oz / ⅓ cup caster
(superfine) sugar
4 egg yolks, beaten

Method

1. Butter the inside of six individual pudding moulds, then coat with brown sugar.

2. Stir the rest of the ingredients together and divide between the pudding moulds.

3. Cover each basin with a square of buttered foil then transfer them to the slow cooker. Pour enough boiling water around them to come halfway up the sides, then cover and cook on high for 3 hours.

4. Turn out the puddings, then caramelise the outsides under a hot grill.

Prune baked custard

Preparation time
20 minutes

Cooking time
3 hours

Serves 6

Ingredients

600 ml / 1 pint / 2 ½ cups
   whole milk
6 large egg yolks
2 tbsp caster (superfine) sugar
150 g / 5 ½ oz / 1 cup prunes,
   pitted

Method

1. Preheat the slow cooker to low. Put the milk in a small saucepan and bring to a boil.

2. Whisk the egg yolks and sugar together, then whisk in the hot milk.

3. Line a baking dish that will fit inside your slow cooker with buttered greaseproof paper and arrange the prunes in the bottom. Pour in the custard mixture, then cover with buttered foil.

4. Put a rack in the slow cooker and pour in 2.5 cm (1 in) of water. Sit the baking dish on top and cook on low for 3 hours, or until the custard is just set with a slight wobble in the centre.

5. Remove the foil and brown the top of the custard under a hot grill before serving.

Smart tip

Look out for
semi-dried Agen
prunes for the
best texture.

Smart tip

Try serving the desserts with shortbread biscuits for added texture.

Pears with crème brûlée

Preparation time
30 minutes

Cooking time
2 hours

Chilling time
1 hour

Serves 4

Ingredients

4 pears, peeled and cored
4 tbsp caster (superfine) sugar
500 ml / 17 ½ fl. oz / 2 cups
    rosé wine
4 star anise
2 cinnamon sticks, halved
4 tbsp runny honey

For the crème brûlée:
450 ml / 12 ½ fl. oz / 1 ¾ cups
    whole milk
4 large egg yolks
75 g / 2 ½ oz / ⅓ cup caster
    (superfine) sugar
2 tsp cornflour (cornstarch)
1 tsp vanilla extract
4 tsp granulated sugar

Method

1. Put the pears, caster sugar, wine and spices in a slow cooker, then cover and cook on medium for 2 hours, turning the pears halfway through.

2. Meanwhile, make the crème brûlée. Pour the milk into a saucepan and bring to boil.

3. Whisk the egg yolks with the caster sugar, cornflour and vanilla extract until thick. Gradually incorporate the hot milk, whisking all the time, then scrape the mixture back into the saucepan.

4. Stir the custard over a low heat until it thickens then divide it between four ramekins.

5. Chill in the fridge for 1 hour, then sprinkle the tops with granulated sugar and caramelise with a blowtorch or under a hot grill.

6. When the pears are ready, drain them of their cooking stock and position on top of the crème brûlée. Spoon the honey over the top to glaze and serve immediately.

Chocolate and berry cakes

Preparation time
30 minutes

Cooking time
2 hours

Serves 6

Ingredients

2 large eggs
125 ml / 4 ½ fl. oz / ½ cup
    sunflower oil
125 ml / 4 ½ fl. oz / ½ cup milk
350 g / 12 ½ oz / 2 ⅓ cups
    self-raising flour, sifted
50 g / 1 ¾ oz / ½ cup
    unsweetened cocoa
    powder, sifted
1 tsp baking powder
200 g / 7 oz / ¾ cup caster
    (superfine) sugar
150 g / 5 ½ oz / 1 cup mixed
    summer berries
icing (confectioners') sugar
    and strawberry leaves
    to garnish

Method

1. Put a rack inside a slow cooker and add 2.5 cm (1 in) of boiling water, then set it to high. Butter 6 mini savarin moulds.

2. Beat the eggs in a jug with the oil and milk until well mixed. Mix the flour, cocoa, baking powder and caster sugar in a bowl, then pour in the egg mixture and stir just enough to combine.

3. Divide the mixture between the moulds and transfer to the slow cooker. Lay 3 layers of kitchen paper over the top of the slow cooker before putting on the lid to absorb the condensing steam.

4. Cook the cakes on high for 2 hours. They are ready when a skewer inserted into the centre comes out clean. Remove the cakes from the slow cooker and leave to cool completely.

5. Turn the cakes out onto plates and fill the centres with berries. Dust with icing sugar and garnish with strawberry leaves.

Smart tip

If you can't find
strawberry leaves to
garnish, use sprigs of
fresh mint instead.

Smart tip

Cooking the pudding in the slow cooker gives it a really velvety texture.

Fruity bread and butter pudding

Preparation time
20 minutes

Cooking time
3 hours

Serves 6

Ingredients

8 slices white bread
4 tbsp butter, softened
100 g / 3 ½ oz / ⅔ cup
    blueberries
50 g / 1 ¾ oz / ⅓ cup
    raspberries
250 ml / 9 fl. oz / 1 cup milk
200 ml / 7 fl. oz / ¾ cup
    double (heavy) cream
4 large egg yolks
75 g / 2 ½ oz / ⅓ cup caster
    (superfine) sugar
1 lemon, zest finely grated
demerara sugar for sprinkling

Method

1. Put a rack inside a slow cooker and add 2.5 cm (1 in) of boiling water, then set it to high. Butter a baking dish that will fit inside the slow cooker.

2. Spread the bread with butter then cut each slice into squares and toss with the blueberries and raspberries in the baking dish.

3. Whisk the milk, cream, eggs, sugar and lemon zest together and pour it over the bread.

4. Cover the pudding with buttered foil, then transfer the dish to the slow cooker. Cover and cook on high for 3 hours or until set with just a slight wobble in the middle.

5. Sprinkle the pudding with demerara sugar and brown the top under a hot grill before serving.

Index

Leeks
Chicken and barley broth, 8
Chicken and carrot pot pies, 124
Chicken and leek pie, 140
Creamy sole with mussels, 52
Fish pie, 135
Haricot bean and vegetable soup, 16
Lamb and vegetable crumble, 163
Leek, potato and avocado soup, 31
Leek, potato and chorizo soup, 23
Mushroom and bacon soup, 15
Rabbit in mustard sauce, 69
Salmon and butter bean blanquette, 66
Spinach, bacon and mushroom pie, 151
Stuffed salmon with leeks, 48
Turkey blanquette, 82
Veal and spinach blanquette, 73

Lemon
Apple and lemon clafoutis, 207
Chicken, lemon and olive stew, 97
Coconut chicken, 131
Fruity bread and butter pudding, 219
Lemon prawns and chicken wings, 42
Lemon yoghurt cake, 176
Pear and apricot compote, 203
Poached fish, 38
Rice pudding with apple and caramel
   compote, 175
Steamed lemon puddings, 208
Strawberry compote with yoghurt cream, 204
Yoghurt panna cotta with sharon fruit
   compote, 180

Lemon curd
Steamed lemon puddings, 208

Lemons, preserved
Chicken, lemon and olive stew, 97
Chorizo, bean and squash stew, 109

Lime
Chorizo, potato and sweetcorn stew, 101
Monkfish curry, 47

Monkfish
Monkfish curry, 47
Seafood and vegetable stew, 78

Mushrooms
Beef, chorizo and mushroom stew, 74
Coq au vin, 70
Creamy veal and wild mushroom casserole, 65
Ham and mushroom cannelloni, 148
Lamb chops with tomato sauce and
   mushroom stew, 94
Mushroom and bacon soup, 15
Salt cod with shrimp and vegetable sauce, 56
Sausage and tomato pasta bake, 156
Sesame chicken and tofu, 44
Spinach, bacon and mushroom pie, 151

Vegetable lasagne, 132

Mussels
Creamy sole with mussels, 52
Curried mussel soup, 19
Seafood and vegetable stew, 78
Tomato and seafood soup, 32

Mustard, dijon
Cauliflower cheese with ham, 159
Creamy sole with mussels, 52
Ham and chicory bake, 152
Rabbit in mustard sauce, 69
Rabbit with baby onions, 89

Mustard, grain
Beef stew with potato gratin topping, 119
Salt cod with shrimp and vegetable sauce, 56

Mustard powder
Coq au vin, 70
Rabbit with baby onions, 89

Nectarines
Poached nectarines with redcurrants, 192

Oats
Lamb and vegetable crumble, 163

Olives
Beef, pepper and olive stew, 81
Chicken, lemon and olive stew, 97
Mediterranean lamb, 106
Ragu pasta bake, 116

Onion
Basque chicken, 77
Beef and pumpkin stew, 113
Beef, pepper and olive stew, 81
Beef stew with potato gratin topping, 119
Cannellini bean and tomato soup, 24
Chicken and sage cannelloni, 128
Chicken and sweetcorn soup, 35
Chicken, rice and vegetable stew, 62
Chicken, lemon and olive stew, 97
Chickpea and chorizo tapas, 85
Chorizo, bean and squash stew, 109
Chunky moroccan lamb soup, 20
Coq au vin, 70
Creamy veal and wild mushroom casserole, 65
Curried mussel soup, 19
Ham, potato and onion pie, 143
Italian sausage meat pie, 160
Lamb and onions with potato gratin
   topping, 136
Lamb and pepper pasta bake, 127
Lamb chops with tomato sauce and
   mushroom stew, 94
Mediterranean lamb, 106
Minestrone with gnocchi, 36

Monkfish curry, 47
Parsnip and yellow split pea soup, 27
Pear, chickpea and vegetable stew, 90
Pepper and tomato soup with meatball
   skewers, 11
Pork and carrot stew, 98
Pork, potato and flageolet stew, 102
Pork with kidney beans, 51
Portuguese salt cod, 40
Rabbit with baby onions, 89
Ragu pasta bake, 116
Ratatouille, 59
Salmon and butter bean blanquette, 66
Salt cod with shrimp and vegetable sauce, 56
Seafood and vegetable stew, 78
Stewed peppers and tomatoes, 86
Tartiflette, 123
Tomato and seafood soup, 32
Topside with caramelised onions, 93
Tuna ragu for pasta, 55
Vegetable bake, 120
Vegetable lasagne, 132
Vegetable tagine, 110

Orange
Apricot and orange compote custards, 195
Orange and almond cake, 191
Pear, chickpea and vegetable stew, 90
Seafood, orange and vegetable stew, 105

Pancetta
Coq au vin, 70

Parsnips
Parsnip and yellow split pea soup, 27

Pasta
Chicken and sage cannelloni, 128
Chorizo and squash pasta bake, 147
Ham and mushroom cannelloni, 148
Lamb and pepper pasta bake, 127
Ragu pasta bake, 116
Sausage and tomato pasta bake, 156
Tuna ragu for pasta, 55
Vegetable lasagne, 132

Pastry, puff
Chicken and carrot pot pies, 124
Chicken and leek pie, 140
Ham, potato and onion pie, 143
Italian sausage meat pie, 160
Spinach, bacon and mushroom pie, 151

Peaches
Lemon yoghurt cake, 176

Pearl barley
Chicken and barley broth, 8

Strawberries
Strawberry compote with yoghurt cream, 204

Strawberry sauce
Condensed milk sponge cake, 196

Stout, irish
Beef stew with potato gratin topping, 119

Sugar snap peas
Seafood, orange and vegetable stew, 105

Sweetcorn
Chicken and sweetcorn soup, 35
Chorizo, potato and sweetcorn stew, 101
Sausage and tomato pasta bake, 156

Tofu
Sesame chicken and tofu, 44

Tomatoes
Basque chicken, 77
Cannellini bean and tomato soup, 24
Cheese, tomato and potato bake, 139
Chickpea and chorizo tapas, 85
Chorizo and squash pasta bake, 147
Chunky moroccan lamb soup, 20
Lamb and pepper pasta bake, 127
Lamb, aubergine and tomato bake, 144
Minestrone with gnocchi, 36
Pepper and tomato soup with meatball
   skewers, 11
Pork and carrot stew, 98
Portuguese salt cod, 40
Ratatouille, 59
Sausage and tomato pasta bake, 156
Stewed peppers and tomatoes, 86
Stuffed salmon with leeks, 48
Tomato and aubergine parmigiana, 155
Tuna ragu for pasta, 55
Vegetable lasagne, 132
Vegetable tagine, 110

Tomato passata
Chorizo and squash pasta bake, 147
Chorizo, bean and squash stew, 109
Chorizo, potato and sweetcorn stew, 101
Lamb chops with tomato sauce and
   mushroom stew, 94
Pork, potato and flageolet stew, 102
Ratatouille, 59
Tomato and seafood soup, 32

Tomato purée
Basque chicken, 77
Beef and pumpkin stew, 113
Beef, pepper and olive stew, 81
Italian sausage meat pie, 160
Minestrone with gnocchi, 36

Pepper and tomato soup with meatball
   skewers, 11
Pork and carrot stew, 98
Portuguese salt cod, 40
Ragu pasta bake, 116
Seafood and vegetable stew, 78
Topside with caramelised onions, 93

Tuna
Tuna ragu for pasta, 55

Turkey
Turkey blanquette, 82

Vanilla
Caramelised rice puddings, 211
Condensed milk sponge cake, 196
Pear and apricot compote, 203
Pears with crème brulee, 215
Rice pudding with apple and caramel
   compote, 175
Vanilla cheesecake, 172
Vanilla poached cherries, 200

Veal
Creamy veal and wild mushroom casserole, 65
Veal and spinach blanquette, 73

Vegetarian mince
Vegetable bake, 120

Walnuts
Baked apples, 168

Watercress
Cauliflower and watercress soup, 12

Wine, red
Coq au vin, 70
Ragu pasta bake, 116

Wine, rice
Sesame chicken and tofu, 44

Wine, rosé
Pears with crème brulee, 215
Vanilla poached cherries, 200

Wine, white
Basque chicken, 77
Chicken and sage cannelloni, 128
Chorizo and squash pasta bake, 147
Creamy sole with mussels, 52
Lamb and onions with potato gratin
   topping, 136
Lamb and pepper pasta bake, 127
Lamb chops with tomato sauce and
   mushroom stew, 94
Mediterranean lamb, 106
Poached fish, 38

Rabbit with baby onions, 89
Ratatouille, 59
Sausage and tomato pasta bake, 156
Seafood and vegetable stew, 78
Seafood, orange and vegetable stew, 105

Yoghurt
Lemon yoghurt cake, 176
Pear and apricot compote, 203
Strawberry compote with yoghurt cream, 204
Yoghurt panna cotta with sharon fruit
   compote, 180